This is the first book devoted to the subject of reconnaissance in the nascent Tank Corps in the Great War. It is a neglected field in spite of passing references to reconnaissance in a number of early books on the history of the Tank Corps. This is also the first attempt to provide a conceptual framework in which to consider intelligence and reconnaissance work and to see it in the broader context of military reconnaissance. Adding the term 'Reconography' to the military lexicon draws attention to a little-known monograph on the subject which has never entered the popular domain before now. The introduction of the tanks on the Western Front in 1916 launched a new form of armoured warfare. After their baptism on 15 September 1916, the tanks became dependent on a few Reconnaissance Officers to guide them into action. The importance of these officers was fully recognised within the Tank Corps itself, but less so outside. The Reconnaissance Officers came to form an elite group of talented men, a special caste, whose contribution to the nascent Tank Corps was far greater than their numbers might suggest. It is surprising, therefore, that the contribution made by these officers has hitherto been neglected in the historiography of British tank operations in the First World War. This book aims to appeal at a number of levels: it seeks to pull together the activities, skills and techniques of tank Intelligence and Reconnaissance Officers and assess their place and contribution to British tank operations in the Great War; it places tank reconnaissance work in the wider context of intelligence and reconnaissance activities prior to the war and it also provides a case study of the tensions that inevitably occur when new wine is put into old bottles, or more prosaically, new technology into existing organisations. It has been necessary to create conceptual structures in which reconnaissance operations can be analysed; it attempts to breathe life into what some might regard as a dull technical subject by devoting space to key figures in Tank Corps' intelligence and reconnaissance activities. Fortunately, and perhaps as a consequence of their activities, they were some of the most colourful and interesting figures in the Tank Corps at that time. In awarding the author the Western Front Association – Helion Holmes Prize, the judges concluded that 'his work reflects deep research, a high standard of writing and a notable originality.'

The book draws together work the author has undertaken in three different academic fields. Colin Hardy graduated from the University of Leeds with a Degree in Geography – having specialised in Geomorphology and Historical Geography. During his study for a MEd at Nottingham University, he specialised in Organisational Theory. The work for both of these Degrees contributed to his election as a Fellow of the Royal Geographical Society (FRGS). Following 35 years in education – retiring as the head teacher of a large secondary school – Colin completed a Master of Arts Degree in British First World War Studies at Birmingham University – and the subject of his dissertation is the basis of this book. He has contributed articles to a number of journals, which have included challenging the conventional wisdom that one of the first tank commanders committed suicide.

Reconographers

Intelligence and Reconnaissance in British Tank Operations on the Western Front 1916–18

Wolverhampton Military Studies No.26

Colin Hardy

Helion & Company Limited

Helion & Company Limited
26 Willow Road
Solihull
West Midlands
B91 1UE
England
Tel. 0121 705 3393
Fax 0121 711 4075
Email: info@helion.co.uk
Website: www.helion.co.uk
Twitter: @helionbooks
Visit our blog http://blog.helion.co.uk/

Published by Helion & Company 2016
Designed and typeset by Mach 3 Solutions Ltd (www.mach3solutions.co.uk)
Cover designed by Paul Hewitt, Battlefield Design (www.battlefield-design.co.uk)
Printed by Lightning Source Ltd, Milton Keynes, Buckinghamshire

Text © Colin Hardy 2016
Images © as individually credited
Maps drawn by George Anderson © Helion & Company Ltd 2016

Every reasonable effort has been made to trace copyright holders and to obtain their permission for the use of copyright material. The author and publisher apologize for any errors or omissions in this work, and would be grateful if notified of any corrections that should be incorporated in future reprints or editions of this book.

Front cover: One newspaper's melodramatic reconstruction of Hotblack guiding a single tank in November 1916 with his highly polished boots (TCMA). Rear cover: Strategic reconnaissance of Cambrai. Reconogram Drawn by Williams-Ellis (TCWEF).

ISBN: 978-1-911096-34-4

British Library Cataloguing-in-Publication Data.
A catalogue record for this book is available from the British Library.

For details of other military history titles published by Helion & Company Limited contact the above address, or visit our website: http://www.helion.co.uk.

We always welcome receiving book proposals from prospective authors.

For

Val, Clare, Mike, Isabel and India

and

Professor Peter Simkins, M.B.E., F.R.Hist.S.
Scholar, Inspiration, Mentor and Friend

Contents

List of Illustrations

List of Maps

Glossary

Archives

BL	British Library.
BLUL	Brotherton Library University of Leeds.
HPSU	Henriques Papers Southampton University
ICMA	Intelligence Corps Museum & Archives, Chicksands.
NAM	National Army Museum.
IWM	Imperial War Museum.
LHCMA	Liddell Hart Centre for Military Archive.
TCMA	Tank Corps Museum and Archives.
TCWEF	Trustees of the Clough Williams-Ellis Foundation.
TNA	The National Archives.
WCA	Winchester College Archives (Warden and Scholars).

Military

A Day	The day following an attack.
APM	Assistant Provost Marshall.
Approach March	The route undertaken by tanks between the detraining station and the 'jumping-off' (Start) point of an attack.
Appreciations	Reports made following a strategic reconnaissance.
AP rounds	Armour Piercing bullets (see SmK).
A7V	The code name for the German tank (*Sturmpanzerwagen*) taken from the name of the department responsible for its creation: *Allgemeines Kriegsdepartment 7, Abteilung Verkehrswesen* (General War Department 7, Traffic Section).
Battlescape	The landscape (terrain) across which the tanks fought.
BEF	British Expeditionary Force on the Western Front.
Bellying	Lack of traction due to the tank sinking into soft ground.
Corons	Terraces of housing in the mining area of Artois (Gohelle).
CO	Commanding Officer.
Crassier	Mining spoil (slag) heaps.

Cribs	Hexagonal crates of reinforced steel that superseded fascines.
DAA	Deputy Assistant Adjutant.
D.C.M.	Distinguished Conduct Medal.
Ditching	The immobilisation of a tank by falling into a trench or shell crater.
Deployment	The movement of tanks to the front line.
DSO	Distinguished Service Order.
Eyewash	A facetious pun applied to inaccurate intelligence.
Fascines	Bundles of brushwood carried by tanks to drop into trenches to enable the tanks to cross them.
Female Tank	A tank with two machine guns in each sponson.
Fieldwork	Primary reconnaissance by first hand observation.
Form lines	Contour lines that are sketched in as distinct from surveyed.
Fosse	A coalmine in Artois (Gohelle).
FRS 1	Field Service Regulations, Part 1 (Operations).
Geoint	Geospatial Intelligence, a modern term for reconnaissance.
GHQ	General Head Quarters of the BEF.
Graphicacy	A visual means of communicating information.
Going	The nature of the terrain to assist or limit the movement of tanks.
HBMGC	Heavy Branch Machine Gun Corps.
HSMGC	Heavy Section Machine Gun Corps.
HQ	Head Quarters of an army unit in the BEF.
Humint	Human Intelligence, a modern term which includes, reports, interrogation of prisoners.
Intelligence	The process of synthesising, analysing and evaluating reconnaissance information.
IO	An intelligence or reconnaissance officer with the rank of major or above.
Iint	Image Intelligence, a modern term for photographic (air) intelligence.
KBS	Kite Balloon Section.
Kaiserschlacht	The German offensive of 21 March 1918 (Emperor's Battle).
Landship	The original name given to the tank.
Lying-up place	The place where tanks assemble the night before an attack.
Male Tank	A tank with a 6 pounder gun in each sponson.
Mark I-V*	The types of heavy fighting tanks.
MC	Military Cross.
MEBUS	A German term for a fortified building or concrete pill box (*Mannschaft EisenBeton UnterStände*).
MMGC	Motor Machine Gun Corps.
OC	Officer Commanding an army unit.

Office Work	Obtaining information by secondary (reconnaissance) methods, e.g. from maps, photos, reports.
ORs	Other Ranks than commissioned officers.
Panzerschrechen	Tank fright.
Pays	Areas of France with their own unique geography.
Pedology	The study of soils.
Penetrometer	An implement for testing the load bearing capacity of soil.
Puits	The entrances to coalmines in Artois (Gohelle).
QMG	Quarter Master General.
Rallying point (place)	The place where tanks should gather following an attack.
Reconnaissance	The collection of information by primary and secondary means.
Reconogram	A graphical representation of information, e.g. landscape sketches, annotated maps or photos.
Reconography	An umbrella term to include all the activities of Reconnaissance and Intelligence Officers.
RO	Reconnaissance Officer, usually a captain or subaltern.
RTU	Returned To Unit.
Russian sap	A shallow tunnel dug across no man's land.
SmK bullets	A German armour piercing round (*Spitzgeschoss mit StahlKern*).
Sponsons	The gun turrets on either side of fighting tanks.
Spuds	Attachments to tank tracks to enable it to drive over soft surfaces.
Start Point (place)	The place from which tanks commence an attack.
Tankodrome	Locations where tanks assemble in large numbers.
TC	Tank Corps.
Terrain	The physical and human landscape.
Terrain analysis	The scientific exploration of the landscape.
Topography	The physical formation (relief) of the landscape.
Underditching beam	A wooden beam, iron shod at the ends, attached by chains to the top of a tank that can be dropped under the tank's tracks to enable it to escape from bellying.
V.C.	Victoria Cross.
Whippet	A medium three-man tank.
Y day	The day before an attack.
Z day	Zero day of an attack.

Introduction & Acknowledgements

> Every work of history reflects the experiences, beliefs and personality of its writer. But every serious work of history is also a collective enterprise, drawing on the painstaking research and thinking of ... scholars today and far in the past.[1]

The present writer says 'Amen' to that. Some historians, however, may conclude that this book is not simply a work of Military History of the Great War. It is biased towards Military (Historical) Geography. Indeed the adoption of the borrowed label 'Reconography' suggests that it might be a special branch of Military Geography solely concerned with reconnaissance work and applied in this instance to tank operations during the First World War. This writer would plead guilty to the charge. A little over seventy specialist Reconnaissance Officers are identified in this account. Their service covered less than the two years of tank operations and they disappeared from the scene as quickly as they had appeared. Their appointment might be regarded as a temporary expedient on the part of the Tank Corps to counter the reconnaissance problems met by the first tanks during their baptism on 15 September 1916. The excuse for researching Tank Corps reconnaissance activities is the recognition that while the introduction of the tanks on the Western Front launched a new form of warfare (armoured) the tanks were dependent on those few Reconnaissance Officers to guide them into action. The importance of these officers was fully recognised within the Tank Corps. The Reconnaissance Officers came to form an elite group of talented men, a special caste, whose contribution to the nascent Tank Corps was far greater than their numbers might suggest. It is, therefore, surprising that the contribution made by these officers has hitherto been generally neglected in the historiography of British tank operations in the First World War. The wish to remedy this neglect might be reason enough to research their work. But there are others.

This subject represents the consummation of the writer's own academic and independent studies. It draws together concepts acquired over the years through formal studies in Geography, Military History together with Organisational and Systems Theory. It is a somewhat extravagant and wrong-headed claim that 'historians that write about war and the military should have worn a uniform at some point in their

---

1   Robert Tombs, *The English and Their History*, (London, Penguin Books Ltd, 2014), p. 4.

lives-be their service ever so humble.'[2] This writer's military Service was very humble indeed since it comprised membership of the University Training Corps (UTC), rising to the lofty heights of corporal after passing Certificate B, and National Service Basic Training at the Intelligence Corps' Depot at Maresfield, Sussex. There one was acquainted with fire and movement in the Ashdown Forest, 'musketry' on the Pevensey Levels'; dish washing in the 'grease pit' of the Cook House and a beer at the 'Chequers' public house before the government decided it needed teachers more than it needed soldiers. There is a third and more nebulous reason to explain the attraction of this subject: curiosity. The point can be clearly identified when this writer was first drawn into a vortex of curiosity that has eventually led to this monograph. The discovery in the 1901 census of an additional cousin, born in 1896, to my maternal family, was immediately followed by a moment of serendipity. The Commonwealth War Graves Commission's web site recorded that 17556 Lance Corporal Cyril Heathcote, 1st Battalion Leicestershire Regiment was killed in action on 15 September 1916 aged 19 and that he is commemorated on the Thiepval Memorial to the Missing. There was a moment of sudden irrational guilt: I had discovered him and killed him in less than half an hour. In expiation I needed to discover more. Minutes before Cyril 'went over the top' and to his death the Battalion history records that he would have witnessed a single tank lumbering towards the Quadrilateral. This was a strong German position between Ginchy and Morval, that the 'Tigers' were about to attack.[3] The solitary tank he observed was commanded by Lieutenant Basil Henriques. This was a surname familiar to the writer from his university days and was a coincidence warranting further research. The tank commander (Basil) was not the Head of the university department as one had wondered although their surname linked them both to the West Indies. However, Basil, five months after his baptism into armoured warfare as a commander of one of the first tanks, became a Tank Corps Reconnaissance Officer.

The opportunity to employ knowledge gained in academic studies together with an inveterate curiosity occurred when a dissertation was a requirement for an MA in British First World War Studies at the University of Birmingham in 2012. Intelligence and reconnaissance in the Tank Corps was a subject that appeared at the time that no one had so far attempted to research. Later I learned that a professional Military Historian, Dr James Beach, had in fact prepared a chapter which sketched out this subject for a book that was awaiting publication and which he generously was prepared to share with me. However, Dr Beach encouraged me to pursue independently my research and advised against reading his draft chapter beforehand. The publication of his work would be sometime after the submission of my dissertation. His wise counsel was adopted. After the MA result had been declared Dr Beach

2   Donald Graves, quoted in Kenneth Radley, *Get Tough, Stay Tough: Shaping the Canadian Corps 1914-1918* (Solihull, Helion & Coy Ltd, 2014), p. 354.
3   H.C. Wylly, *History of the 1st & 2nd Battalions the Leicestershire Regiment in the Great War* (Aldershot, Gale & Polden Ltd, no date), p. 35.

and I exchanged chapter and dissertation. It was unsurprising that our independent research overlapped since we had drawn on a number of similar sources. I confess to being particularly jealous of his superbly imaginative title: *Scouting for Brigands*.[4] Dr Beach, however, made the shrewd observation that whilst he had approached the subject 'top down' with a particular focus on wider Tank Corps intelligence, the dissertation had adopted a 'bottom up' approach with its greater emphasis on 'the reconnaissance imperative'.[5]

Both works acknowledge a particular debt to Dr Bryn Hammond. His thesis on *The Theory and Practice of Cooperation with Other arms on the Western Front during the First World War* is fundamental to any understanding of the Tank Corps. Although the thesis is available on-line it deserves a wider audience. I wish to acknowledge the valuable advice I received from both these professionals. I would further add the names of two other 'Young Turks' of the academic establishment. Dr Spencer Jones for his knowledge regarding pre-First World War reconnaissance together with his generosity of advice and Dr Michael LoCicero for his encouragement in writing this account.

This book aims to appeal at a number of levels. It seeks to pull together the activities, skills and techniques of tank Intelligence and Reconnaissance Officers and assess their place and contribution to British tank operations in the Great War. It places tank reconnaissance work in the wider context of intelligence and reconnaissance activities prior to the war. It also provides a case study of the tensions that inevitably occur when new wine is put into old bottles, or more prosaically, new technology into existing organisations. It attempts to breathe life into what some might regard as a dull technical subject by devoting space to key figures in Tank Corps' intelligence and reconnaissance activities, the Reconographers of the title. Fortunately, and perhaps as a consequence of their activities, they were some of the most colourful and interesting figures in the Tank Corps at that time. It is also important to be reminded that 'it was not the tank, not the gun; but the man' that was the critical element in military operations.[6]

Chapter One draws attention to and speculates on the reasons for the absence in the historiography of the Tank Corps of the importance of the work the Intelligence and Reconnaissance Officers. Chapter Two uses the Tank Corps terminology of 'The Approach March' as a metaphor to explain the specific approach taken in this account of Intelligence and Reconnaissance operations and particularly why it does not follow a chronological (historical) route to tank operations in the First World War. A discussion occurs in Chapter Three of the key terms 'Reconography', 'Intelligence' and

---

4   James Beach, 'Scouting for Brigands: British Tank Corps Reconnaissance and Intelligence' in *Genesis,Employment and Aftermath, First World War Tanks and the New Warfare*, Aleric Searle (ed.), (Solihull, Helion & Company Limited, 2015). The book was published three years later.
5   Ibid., p. 109.
6   Paddy Griffith, *Forward into Battle*, (Swindon, Croward Press, 1990 [1981], p. 119.

'Reconnaissance' in the context of tank operations. It is not the intention in Chapter Four to offer a potted history of the early days of the Tank Corps although it inevitably refers to this period in the context of the career of one of the original Tank Commanders. This proved to be an initial and decisive step leading to his appointment as a Company then Battalion Reconnaissance Officer. It is also the opportunity to explain the original nomenclatures of the Corps during his period of service. A case study in Chapter Five of the baptism of the tanks on 15 September 1916 describes the inadequate reconnaissance activities that made it necessary to appoint the specialist Intelligence and Reconnaissance Officers. The establishment of a specialist Reconnaissance Department within the nascent Tank Corps provides the opportunity to consider in Chapter Six the activities of the legendary and colourful Officer Commanding (O.C.) the Tank Intelligence and Reconnaissance Department. It was he who set the standards for the Department and promoted its *esprit d'corps*. The chapter that follows entitled 'The Gifted Amateurs' deals with the appointment of these specialist officers. It describes their place in the organisational structure of the Tank Corps. The 'Growing Pains' outlined in Chapter Eight considers how pragmatic considerations overcame any initial doctrine regarding the responsibilities for reconnaissance and suggests how the Reconnaissance Officers came to be regarded by other tank officers as members of a high caste within the Corps. This is also the opportunity to propose a model of their reconnaissance role based upon an analysis of their activities. The next four chapters, nine through twelve, use the model as a framework in which to detail and illustrate their operational responsibilities for Reconnaissance Training, Preparatory (Strategic and Tactical) Reconnaissance, Battle (Combat) Reconnaissance and Protective Reconnaissance. The final chapter aims to summarise Tank Corps' Intelligence and Reconnaissance activities. An added postscript considers the post war careers of the key personalities who have been used to illustrate these operations.

The present writer gratefully acknowledges the assistance of many other people who have directly and indirectly contributed to this work. I thank the archive and library staff of the Special Collections in the Brotherton Library, the University of Leeds; The Liddell Hart Collection at King's College; the Tank Corps Museum and Archive at Bovington, Dorset; the Intelligence Corps Museum and Archive at Chicksands, Bedfordshire; the Imperial War Museum; National Army Museum and the Royal Geographical Society. I offer my grateful thanks to the Trustees of the Clough Williams-Ellis Trust for allowing the reproduction of quotations and drawings of Sir Clough Williams-Ellis. There are a number of individuals to whom I am particularly indebted. These include the late Rabbi Lawrence Rigal and Ms Jane Henriques for helping me to understand the life and work of Basil Henriques and Geoffrey V. Hotblack for offering both insights and evidence of the later military career of his great uncle, Frederick Elliot Hotblack, as well as Lieutenant Colonel (Rtd.) Geoffrey Vesey Holt and Lieutenant Colonel Jeffery Schnakenberg (USAAF) for information about the contemporary Armour and Intelligence scene. I have been delighted with the encouragement and information provided by members of the network of 'Old

Birmingham University Masters Students. In particular, my thanks to Simon Worrall who seems to pull on-line references out of the ether at will. I value the knowledge of members of the Cheltenham and Gloucester Branch of the Western Front Association especially Bob Brunsdon, Gold Badge Battlefield Guide, who meets all the criteria of the first class Reconographer and especially for his finding the 'River' Crinchon amidst the confusion of railways, roads, tracks and housing of metropolitan Arras – Achicourt together with Graham Adams for feeding me information about the tanks. I am grateful to the members of the Great War Forum for supplying answers to my technical questions. This is a reservoir of information I have been able to call upon freely. My thanks also go to Malcolm Lewis for his expert graphical skills and George Anderson for the clarity of the maps. I am also grateful to Captain Oleksandre Dudov, Master of the MV Minerva (Swan Hellenic), for clarifying, over dinner, the working relationship between a ship's commander and an on-board pilot and thereby the relationship between a Tank Commander and Reconnaissance Officer. This may also be the occasion to record my debt to my principal mentors in the Military History of the Great War: Professors Peter Simkins and Gary Sheffield and Dr Spencer Jones and also to Duncan Rogers, proprietor of Helion & Company, for having the courage to publish this book and for the courtesy and patience in responding to my frequently inane questions. Last, but certainly not least, I must publically offer my greatest thanks to my wife, Val, for her encouragement, support and practical assistance during my studies and the writing of this book which is only matched by her horror at discovering a split infinitive and a Greengrocer's apostrophe!

Colin Hardy
Stroud, Gloucestershire
1 September 2015

1

A Gap in the Records

The historiography of the Tanks Corps between 1916 and 1918 appears fairly comprehensive. It includes the origin of the tanks written by Sir Basil Liddell Hart.[1] Trevor Pidgeon details their baptism of fire.[2] Tank Corps successes at Cambrai are described by B. Cooper[3] and their failures during the Third Ypres campaign by R. Prior and T. Wilson.[4] In his unpublished PhD thesis Dr Bryn Hammond analyses the Tank Corps' co-operation with other arms.[5] There were controversies surrounding the origin and employment of tanks with which J. P. Harris has dealt which includes a critical appraisal of the work of both Liddell Hart and J.F.C. Fuller.[6] David Fletcher described individual tank actions.[7] The French researchers, Gibot and Gorczyynski, have also described individual tank actions at Cambrai.[8] Likewise Somers detailed the operations of the 6th Tank Battalion which included the employment of the Medium Tank or 'Whippet' but unfortunately his wealth of detail is not helped by the absence of maps.[9] Reassessment of the successful tank action at Cambrai has also been made by Hammond.[10] There are as well a number of general histories of

1   B. H. Liddell Hart, *The Tanks, Volume One, 1914-1939* (London, Cassell, 1959), pp. 3-48.
2   T. Pidgeon, *The Tanks at Flers* (Cobham, Fairmile Books, 1995).
3   B. Cooper, *The Ironclads of Cambrai* (Barnsley, Pen & Sword Military, 2010 [1967]).
4   R. Prior & T Wilson, *Passchendaele, The Untold Story* (New Haven & London, Yale University Press, 2002 [1996].
5   C. B. Hammond, *Theory and Practice of Tank Cooperation with other Arms on the Western Front during the First World War*, (Unpublished PhD thesis, University of Birmingham, 2005.
6   J. P. Harris, *Men, Ideas and Tanks, British Military Thought and Armoured Forces, 1903-1939* (Manchester, Manchester University, 1995).
7   David Fletcher, *Tanks and Trenches* (Stroud, Sutton Publishing, undated).
8   J.L. Gibot & P. Gorczynski, *Follow the Tanks, Cambrai, 20 November-7 December 1917* (Arras, Imprimerie Centrale de Artois, trans. McAdam, W., 1999).
9   A.H.T. Somers, *The War History of the Sixth Tank Battalion*, (Uckfield, The Naval & Military press Ltd., reprinted & undated.
10 B. Hammond, *Cambrai 1917* (London, Weidenfeld & Nicolson, 2008).

the Tank Corps in the First World War of which the husband and wife team of Clough and Amabel Williams-Ellis was the first in 1919.[11] Even Tank Corps myths are perpetuated, for instance, the allegation in the official history that in the opening Tank action at Ginchy Henriques' tank fired on the 9th Norfolks.[12] Trevor Pidgeon, after a forensic examination of the evidence, convincingly demonstrates that it was a misinterpretation of events.[13] There is also the allegation of the suicide of Lieutenant George Macpherson on the opening day of the Flers-Courcelette battle.[14] This has been challenged by the present writer.[15] Ironically even the distinguished revisionist Military Historian, John Terraine, in seeking to dispose of myths about the employment of Tanks, repeats this particular fiction.[16] The technical enthusiasts have their authors particularly David Fletcher, formerly archivist at the Tank Corps Museum and Archives at Bovington.[17] This historiographical list also includes tank apologists, not the least Major, later Major General, J.F.C. Fuller by whom German General Heinz Guderian set great store.[18]

Tank enthusiasts would have to search diligently to find references to Reconnaissance Officers (ROs) in the literature. Watson makes a passing reference to the unidentified 'Jumbo, my reconnaissance officer.' Somers, Commander of the 6th Tank Battalion and Hickey, a Section Commander, also refer to anonymous Reconnaissance Officers.[19] More specific references are found when the authors, Henriques, Browne and Williams-Ellis have themselves served as ROs.[20] Many of these authors, mostly writing before the Second World War and who generally served in the earlier conflict, provide both an authenticity and useful pointers to the work of the ROs. However, considerable care has to be taken in using their work. For instance, readers would fail to appreciate that at least forty ROs were engaged on 20 November, 1917 at Cambrai.[21]

11   C. & A. William-Ellis, et al, *The Tank Corps* (London: Country life, 1919).
12   Wilfred Miles, *Military Operations in France and Belgium 1916, Volume 2*, (Uckfield, Naval & Military Press, reprint of 1938 edition), p. 310.
13   Pidgeon, *Tanks at Flers*, pp. 59-60.
14   Campbell, Christy, *Band of Brigands* (London: Harper Press, 2007), p. 203.
15   Colin Hardy, 'Rewriting History-An Alternative Account of the Death of Lieutenant George Macpherson of the Heavy Section Machine Gun Corps', *Stand To! The Journal of the Western Front Association*, (August/September 2010, Number 89, pp. 30-32).
16   John Terraine, *The Smoke and the Fire* (London, Sigwick & Jackson, 1980), p. 149.
17   D. Fletcher, *The British Tanks 1915-19* (Marlborough, Crowood Press Ltd., 2001).
18   J.F.C. Fuller, *Tanks in the Great War 1914-1918*. Heinz Guderian, *Achtung – Panzer! The Development of Tank Warfare*, (London, Cassell, 1992 [1937].
19   W. H. L. Watson, *A Company of Tanks* (Edinburgh & London, Blackwood & Sons, 1920), p. 27 and Somers, A. H. T., *The War History of the Sixth Tank Battalion*, Hickey, D. E., *Rolling into Action*, (Uckfield, Naval & Military Press Ltd, undated).
20   B. L. Q. Henriques, *Indiscretions of a Warden* (London, Methuen & Co. Ltd., 1937), D. G. Browne, *The Tank in Action* (London, Blackwood, 1920) and Williams-Ellis, et al, *The Tank Corps*.
21   1 GSO 2, 3rd Brigade ROs, 9 Battalion ROs and 27 Company ROs.

Dr James Beach is the single scholar to focus solely on the activities of Tank Corps Intelligence and Reconnaissance officers in a recent publication.[22]

Frequently the authors combine history, memoir, hindsight and anecdote (often written, like Foley, in the blood and thunder style of *The Boys' Own Paper*).[23] They are not works of scholarship. The frequent lack of foot or end notes means their sources are obscure. There was a reliance on memory of up to ten years or more after the events. Thus Henriques' two accounts of his approach march on the night of 14/15 September, 1916 and subsequent reconnaissance[24] is at variance with the account he gives in his memoir over 20 years later.[25] Occasionally the authors are inaccurate. The William-Ellises quote from a transcription of a lecture given by Henriques but are mistaken in his rank.[26] They continue by quoting 'another Tank Commander' who they do not name when it is clearly also taken from Henriques' lecture. Some authors are both self-promoting and exhibit bias. Former Brigadier General C.D. Baker-Carr, a non-regular officer, believed his contributions were not sufficiently regarded by High Command to warrant further promotion.[27] Unsurprisingly he is extremely critical of GHQ. His judgements, especially praising General Henry Wilson, are controversial.[28] John Terraine dismisses him as 'a silly, conceited brigadier.'[29] These former Tank Corps Officers wrote at a time when their loyalty to the Corps was tested by the doubts raised as to the future of the tanks. Without benefit of the wider picture they are often unfairly critical of higher command, particularly Haig. There was, however, some justification for the belief that the tanks were misunderstood and misused. J.F.C. Fuller and Basil Liddell Hart, whose history of The Tank Corps was sponsored and tailored by the regiment, in particular engaged in polemics in support of armoured operations. These secondary sources and memoirs are laced with bias in favour of the tanks which could render them of limited value. Browne is tendentious when he writes 'if it sounds extravagant to claim the tanks won the war, it is indisputable that they hastened its end by six months or a year. The final advance would have been impossibility (sic) without them.'[30] It would, however, be a mistake, in spite of the above criticisms, to dismiss them completely. Amongst the opinions, special pleading and

22 James Beach, 'Scouting for Brigands: British Tank Corps Reconnaissance and Intelligence, 1916-1918' in A. Searle (ed), *Genesis, Employment and Aftermath* (Solihull, Helion Press, 2015).
23 R. Foley, *The Boilerplate War*, pp. 92-113.
24 B. L. Q. Henriques, 'Untitled Report of 17 September 1916' (Tank Corps Museum & Archives). B. L. Q. Henriques, 'Attack on the Quadrilateral' (a transcription of a lecture with hand written amendments delivered on the 6 March 1917, Tank Corps Museum & Archives).
25 Henriques, *Indiscretions of a Warden*, pp. 117-118.
26 Henriques, B. L. Q. Record of Service (Glasgow, Army Personnel Centre).
27 C. D. Baker-Carr, *From Chauffeur to Brigadier* (London, Ernest Benn Ltd., 1930).
28 Ibid., p. 270.
29 Terraine, *The Smoke and the Fire*, p. 141.
30 Browne, *The Tank in Action*, p. 14.

bias there is considerable factual information. Often the facts can be cross-referenced and authenticated or contradicted as the case may be in unit documents and War Diaries. Even these primary sources can be self-serving and unhelpful by identifying Reconnaissance Officers by their role ('RO') rather than by their names.

Although unit diaries may not refer to specific ROs, some include after-action reports written and signed by them which indicate, in passing, the type of activities in which they were engaged and the difficulties they faced. F.G. Maurice in his *Tank Corps Book of Honour* is particularly valuable since he lists the names of those Reconnaissance Officers together with their Units who were awarded decorations. The citations also describe their activities.[31] They help, together with 'Order of Battle 1918'[32] and unit war diaries, to identify a number of the ROs.[33] There are very few later studies that use primary sources to focus on specific tank units and to refer to the work of the RO. An exception is Ian Verrinder in his book *Tanks in Action in the Great War, B Battalion's Experiences 1917*.[34] He employs the unit war diary and the accounts (both verbal and written) of tank RO, Captain (later Colonel) Norman Musgrave (Mark) Dillon, to chronicle one Tank Battalion's experiences but only in 1917. Dillon's accounts are archived at the University of Leeds, the Imperial War Museum and the Army Museum.

This gap in the historiography of the Tank Corps seems at first surprising since the work of the Intelligence and Reconnaissance Officers was highly regarded. J.F.C. Fuller claims 'tank operations require the most careful preparation and minute reconnaissance in order to render them successful.'[35] F. Mitchell saw reconnaissance as 'that most important subject.'[36] C.D. Baker-Carr opined that the Tank Corps' Reconnaissance Department was 'not only necessary; it was a matter of life and death' and 'good reconnaissance work was the foundation of all success.'[37] Browne remarked that 'there were contingencies that affected no other arm. Especially was this the case with reconnaissance; for success or failure hung upon the tank commanders' familiarity, from thorough coaching beforehand, with the ground they had to cover.'[38] As early as 11 June 1916 Lieutenant Colonel John Brough, Colonel Swinton's representative at General Head Quarters (GHQ), emphasised that 'reconnaissance is essential.'[39] Reconnaissance was a 'force multiplier.' The subject may have been neglected because

31   R. F. G. Maurice, *Tank Corps Book of Honour* (Ballantyre, Spottiswood, 1919), pp. 71-234.
32   TCMA, the 'Order of Battle' only names the Brigade and Battalion ROs.
33   See Appendix I.
34   I. Verrinder, *Tank Action in the Great War: B Battalion's Experiences 1917* (Barnsley, Pen & Sword Military, 2009).
35   Fuller, *Tanks in the Great War 1914-1918*, p. 59.
36   F. Mitchell, *Tank Warfare: The Story of the Tanks in the Great War* (London, T. Nelson & Sons, 1933), p. 86.
37   Baker-Carr, *From Chauffeur to Brigadier*, pp. 193, 211.
38   Browne, *Tank in Action*, p. 54.
39   TNA, WO158/834 Military HQ: Correspondence & papers, January 1916-August 1916, 'Tactical Employment of Tanks' (June-August 1916).

Intelligence and Reconnaissance contributes to the less dramatic logistics of the Tank Corps. It is a part of the 'tail', albeit one which had a sting in it during the German March Offensive of 1918, rather than the popular 'tooth' of the Tank Corps. Intelligence and reconnaissance, like the supply, maintenance, repair and recovery of tanks falls into that 'unglamorous' and technical but vital part of the army's support echelons that also includes the Army Service Corps and Engineers.[40] None figure prominently in the popular historiography of the First World War although it has been remarked that 'professionals talk logistics and intelligence.'[41] A further explanation might be that 'all the 1916-18 Reconnaissance stuff was sent to Bovington and had, later, to be drastically weeded out on account of lack of storage space.'[42] The establishment of the Intelligence and Reconnaissance Department might also be regarded as only a temporary expedient since it existed for only two years and was established to meet very specific circumstances arising from the baptism of the tanks on 15 September 1916 and positional warfare. Not long after the Armistice 'the Reconnaissance School was closed up, its need having gone.'[43] The aim of this account is to help fill this gap in the history of the Tank Corps.

40   Major John Pratt, 'An Analysis of the Effectiveness of Tank Maintenance, Repair and Recovery Work on the Western Front 1916 to 1918', (unpublished dissertation, University of Birmingham, 2013).
41   Quoted by John Hughes-Wilson, *History of the First World War in 100 Objects*, (London, Cassel, 2014), p. 304.
42   Liddell Hart Centre for Military Archives (LHCMA), 9/28/43, Letter from Hotblack to Liddell Hart, 22 March 1948.
43   Brotherton Library, University of Leeds (BLUL), M. N. Dillon Report, p. 27.

2

The 'Approach March'

The subject of intelligence and reconnaissance in tank operations will be approached thematically rather than chronologically. The reader will not find here a sequential account of reconnaissance operations beginning with the baptism of the tanks on the Somme on the 15 September 1916 before moving on to the four major tank engagements of 1917: the Battle of Arras beginning on 9 April followed by the attack on the Messines Ridge (7 June), Third Ypres (31 July) and Cambrai (20 November). In 1918 successful tank offensives took place at Hamel (4 July), Amiens (8-12 August) to be followed by Tank operations during the '100 Days' that included the Battles of Albert-Arras (21 August-3 September), the Cambrai-Hindenburg Line (18 September-10 October) and the final battles associated with crossing the rivers Selle and Sambre (17 October-11 November). Before the 1918 actions Reconnaissance Officers also had to prepare for and face the German Spring Offensive (*Kaiserschlacht*) that began on 21 March 1918.

Inevitably there will be frequent references to these tank operations and to individual Reconnaissance Officers in so far as they illustrate the multiple tasks that faced the Intelligence and Reconnaissance Department. A chronological approach would not demonstrate any obvious 'learning curve' or learning process although after action reports included recommendations for future operations. There was a major step change in the development of their activities after the Somme operations in 1916 which led to their greater effectiveness. The Reconnaissance Department benefitted from this experience and that inherited from a long military tradition of tried and tested methods in reconnaissance. It will, therefore, be useful to outline this heritage particularly in the decades prior to the outbreak of the First World War. This approach will show how initially this fund of experience and advice was largely ignored but then eventually led to the establishment of the specialist Tank Corps Intelligence and Reconnaissance Department. The success of this Department, which had no specific tank reconnaissance doctrine, lay more in a pragmatic adaption of reconnaissance to four critical elements relevant in all military operations: **Technology** (the tanks and the characteristics of this new weapon which they supported); **Terrain** (the 'battlescapes' across which tanks had to operate),**Tactics** (the changes in the military operations that employed tanks) and **Training** (of tank and unit commanders for specific operations).[1]

Technology: as has already been indicated, the mechanical details of tanks together with their technical improvements over the two years of their operation can be found elsewhere. However, it is valuable here to focus on the technology of the tank only insofar as it was a 'fixed variable' which affected its ergonomics and which in turn was an important consideration for the work of the Reconnaissance Officers. This reinforces Bryn Hammond's view that the mechanical characteristics of the Tank profoundly affected all their actions.[2] The Tank enthusiast can point to the improvements to the Tank that took place between the original Mark I of 1916 and the Mark V* (Star) of 1918. The rear hydraulic stabilizers (stub axles) were unnecessary and removed. The protective armour of the Mark IV Tank was increased and made thicker than in the Mark I that had proved vulnerable to armour piercing (AP) bullets. The sponsons were reduced in size and could be retracted so they no longer had to be unbolted when entraining. Metal attachments, 'spuds', could be fixed to tank tracks to assist them across soft ground (but if not removed could damage road surfaces). The 'unditching beam' was an asset when released from the roof of the tanks to assist them to escape from shell craters and trenches as long as it was not attempted under sustained machine gun fire.

The greatest improvement was in the Mark V driving system. The tank no longer needed two 'gears men' and a driver to manoeuvre it. The engine was improved as the150 horse power Ricardo replaced the 105 horse power Daimler although exhaust fumes could flood the interior with carbon monoxide. The gravity feed of petrol to the engine was replaced by an 'autovac' system. In spite of these improvements 'the Tanks were still very primitive.'[3] The General Service Officer, 2, (Intelligence) (GSO2 [I]) responsible for the Reconnaissance Branch described the Mark IV Tank some years later as still 'in an early stage of development and suffering from many teething troubles and that it was a Frightener rather than a Fighter.'[4] This mirrored German Quartermaster-General Erich Ludendorff's concern about *Panzerschrechen* (tank fright). In fact the tank was mechanically unreliable with a very high consumption of petrol of two miles to the gallon. The location of supply dumps were critical since 'for 1 day of 10 running hours each tank would require 70 gallons of petrol, 5 gallons of engine oil, 40 gallons of water and 7 pounds of grease.'[5] Thus 'careful Reconnaissances

1   There may be a case for adding these 4Ts to other military alliterations: the 2Fs (fog and friction) and3Cs (command, control and communications).
2   Hammond, *Theory and Practice of Tank Cooperation with other Arms*, p. 380.
3   Brotherton Library (Special Collections), University of Leeds (BLUL), Record of N. M. Dillon, p.17.
4   Intelligence Corps Museum (ICM), F. E. Hotblack Recollections, Confidential, B. B. C. T.V. Programme on Tanks, no accession number, 1971, p.2.
5   Harris, *Men, Ideas and Tanks*, p. 91.

The Mark I Tank later Marks differed little in shape, size and weight. (TCMA)

The medium Tank (the 'Whippet). (TCMA)

are as essential for Supply as Fighting Tanks.'[6] The Mark I's weight (28 tons), size (9.91 m. × 4.19m × 2.49 m.) and distinctive lozenge shape, slowness (average 3 mph) and poor manoeuvrability made it vulnerable particularly to artillery (the Medium Tank, the 'Whippet' of 1918, was 5 mph faster and weighed in at 14 tons). The tracks of the heavy tank could destroy road surfaces, water pipelines, telephone poles and wires and leave distinctive tracks that could be observed by enemy aircraft. It was

6   Ibid., p. 100.

helpless in very soft and shell torn ground and woods. The early tanks could rarely travel more than fifteen miles before they required some form of mechanical service. The restricted vision of the tanks limited observation and navigation. The tank's steel structure affected compasses. The noise, heat, vibration and physical effort exhausted the crew and limited the amount of time they could operate. Hence route finding also included suitable 'half-way houses' for resting *en route*. A tank driver, Corporal (later Second Lieutenant) William Taylor Dawson, graphically describes this experience in a Mark IV tank during Third Ypres:

> I had been in the driving seat for 13 hours without moving out and of course nothing to eat or drink. During the return journey, owing to the many hundreds (possibly even thousands) of times I had to operate the clutch to enable the track gears to be changed for the purpose of steering clear of obstacles or bad patches of ground, my thigh muscles in my clutch leg suffered from cramp and exhaustion and I often had to use both legs – a rather awkward and difficult thing to do. The result was that when at last I got out of the tank, my legs gave way and I had to lie down for a while.[7]

Hence a tank often had two crews: one to drive it on the approach march behind the lines and a second fighting crew to take it into battle. There were serious communication problems within the tank, between tanks and with infantry and aircraft that were addressed by waving spades, raising helmets on bayonets, banging on the engine with a spanner followed by hand signs and prodding with walking sticks. Carrier pigeons were used to communicate with HQ and later primitive wirelesses were carried in special signal tanks. However 'the application of wireless to tanks during the First World War can aptly be described as "an experiment inside an experiment".'[8] The claim that the Tanks could go anywhere was a myth. Clearly no past reconnaissance experience, military doctrine or regulations had to consider such factors as these and they prevailed until the armistice.

A second key variable in reconnaissance operations was the **Terrain** or 'battlescape', that is, the landscape or terrain over which the tanks advanced and fought. This is not the place to provide a detailed description of the geography of the landscapes of northern France and Belgium where tank operations took place. However, it has been suggested, that: 'the First World War is ... arguably one of the first modern conflicts in which terrain analysis played a significant role, helping to determine not only the

---

7   Wm Taylor Dawson, Reminiscences of my Experiences in the First Tanks, (C Coy personal papers, TCMA, p. 13).
8   Brian M. Hall, The development of Tank Communications in the British Expeditionary Force, 1916-1918, in Alaric Searle (ed), *Genesis, Employment and Aftermath* (Solihull, Helion & Company Limited, 2015), p. 152.

character, but also the outcome of many of the most important battles'.[9] Whilst Doyle and Bennett concentrate their analysis on positional trench warfare in Flanders and Picardy between November 1914 and December 1917, their thoughts have, by extension, wider implications for tank reconnaissance. Quoting Mitchell and Gavish,[10] they suggest that:

> ... the military assessment of terrain has two aspects; strategic and tactical. Strategic assessment is concerned with the disposition of large scale geographic features such as urban centres, transport systems, lowlands, uplands, sea and river barriers in the planning of military campaigns. Tactical assessments are primarily concerned with detailed aspects of terrain and their direct influence on the outcome of battles.[11]

Strategic and tactical reconnaissance both figure prominently in the work of the Tank Corps Intelligence (IOs) and Reconnaissance Officers (ROs). However, it is sufficient here, to note the contrasts in the terrain across which tanks had to be conducted (the 'going') and fought and accordingly reconnaissance route planning had to consider. In a later paper Doyle emphasises the critical importance of 'the ground conditions in influencing the movement of troops, equipment, and later, **tanks**' (emphasis added).[12] The terrain of the battlescapes included features of both human and physical geography, macro and micro characteristics of landscape and the consequences of weather and climate. This also included the deformation of the landscape as a consequence of earlier or the current battle.

The macro-landscapes ('gross terrain characteristics') across which strategic tank reconnaissance took place were broadly consistent with the principal historical provinces of Flanders (French and Belgian), Artois and Picardy. Tactical reconnaissance was closely related to the French *Pays*.[13] These are small regions (meso-landscapes) within the provinces that are characterized by a unique inter-relationship between the physical and human geography. This is similar to the 'system of compartmenting the terrain into specific areas with similar attribute – called "land systems" by today's military analysts ... typical terrain units, the land systems, are characterised in terms of their geology, geomorphology, surface "going" characteristics, vegetation and

9   Peter Doyle & Matthew R. Bennett, 'Military Geography: terrain evaluation and the British Western Front 1914-1918' in *The Geographical Journal*, Vol. 163 part 1 March 1997).
10   C. W. W Mitchell and D. Gavish, 'Land on which battles are lost or won', *Geographical Magazine*, No. 52, 1980, pp. 838-840.
11   Doyle & Bennett, pp. 2-3.
12   Peter Doyle, 'Geology and the War on the Western Front, 1914-18', *Geology Today*, vol. 30, no. 5, Sept.-Oct. 2014, p.186.
13   Characterization of the *Pays* owes much to the work of the eminent French Geographer Paul Vidal de la Blache (1845-1918).

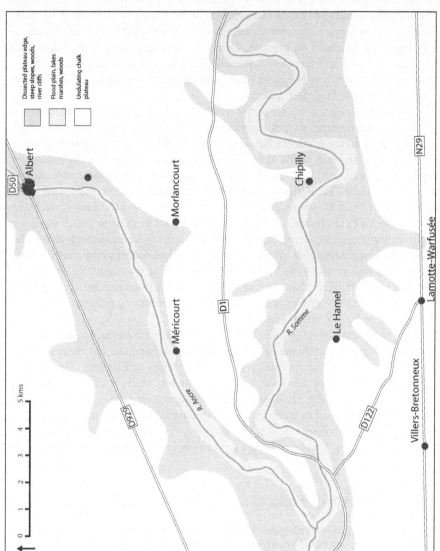

Map 1 Picardy, Somme–Ancre Area: an example of a 'land system'.

hydrogeology – all of which influenced the tactical use of the ground.'[14] Map 1 illustrates a 'land system' in the Somme-Ancre area of Picardy.[15] The map hints at the different terrain of the Fourth Army in which tanks had to operate during the Battle of Amiens, 8 August 1918. The area of operation of III Corps north of the Somme was far more dissected and wooded than the ANZAC Corps' battlescape to the south of the river and was one reason for to their limited success. Eight *Pays* can be identified as tank battlescapes.[16] In practice, however, the Company and Battalion ROs were concerned with the features technically known as 'facets' of the landscape of even more localized micro-landforms and battlescapes, for instance, hill gradients, streams, soils, woods, landmarks, farms.

It was not just along the course of the relatively static north to south front line of 1914-1917 that battlescapes varied, but also across the more mobile west to east fronts in late 1917-1918. In the north the Reconnaissance Officers had to prepare tank routes across the low-lying plain of the Ypres salient composed of Flanders (Ypresian) clay south of the coastal inundated polder land. It was crossed by innumerable streams and drainage ditches 'its flatness relieved only by a series of low hills with elevations no greater than 50 metres'.[17] To the south of Ypres was the low Wytschaete-Messines ridge of Panisellan Sand of the Ghent and Tielt formations which was a part of an arc of higher ground stretching from Staden north of Ypres through Passendale (Passchendaele) and Geluveldt. Mont Kemmel formed an outlier to the south. Within the salient the area south of the Ypres to Zonnebeke road was more densely wooded than to the north. Belgian Flanders had a dispersed settlement pattern of many farms and hamlets which the Germans could turn into multiple strong points (the infamous *Mannschaft EisenBeton Unterstände* or MEBUS).[18]

South of the Messines ridge and the River Lys and as far as the La Bassée Canal (Canal d'Aire) and beneath the slight but critical higher land (10 metres) of the Aubers Ridge is a landscape reminiscent of the fenlands of England. This flat 'wet Flanders plain', crossed by a mosaic of drainage ditches, made it virtually 'tank free' between1916-18. (see map 2) These 'levels' abruptly ends at the La Bassée canal where reconnaissance had to accommodate an industrial landscape of manufacturing towns (Lens), mining villages (Loos, Givenchy) and hamlets (Cité St Elie), terraced housing (*Corons*), deep coal mines (*Fosse*), pit heads (*puits*), spoil heaps (*crassiers*) and

14   P. Chasseaud & P. Doyle, *Grasping Gallipoli*, Stroud, Spellmount History Press, 2015 [2005], p. 3.
15   The map was an exercise undertaken by the present writer and is based upon original primary (observation & fieldwork) and secondary (analysis of map IGN 2408O) 'reconnaissance'.
16   See Appendix II.
17   Doyle, *Geology and the War on the Western Front, 1914-19*, p. 184.
18   See, for instance, the thirteen farms and cottages north of Passchendaele denoted by Dr Michael LoCicero in *A Moonlight Massacre: The Night Operation on the Passchendaele Ridge, 2 December 1917* (Solihull, Helion & Co., 2014).

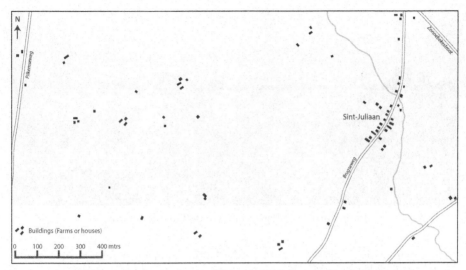

The open landscape north of Ypres with its dispersed settlements.

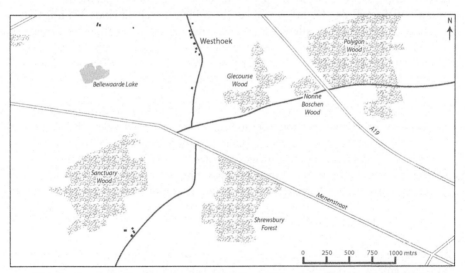

The closely wooded landscape south of the Ypres-Passendale (Passchendaele) Road.

brickstacks (Cuinchy) in Artois. It was not good tank country although a faux tank reconnaissance had been made in the area in February 1917. Simon Peaple, in his discussion about the 46th North Midland's operation in the Lens sector on 1 July 1917, notes that German gunners on 'the high ground provided by railway embankments and two built up areas' would 'have picked off British tanks moving at one mile

The industrial-mining area of Artois. (Gohelle) (Author)

an hour with ease.'[19] This did not prevent XI Corps commander, Lieutenant General Sir Richard Haking, in March whilst planning the attack toying with the idea of using at least one tank since 'the news of its arrival might be spread to the enemy and we could also test it in this muddy ground with a view to future operations.'[20]

South of Vimy Ridge (a fault scarp) lay the rolling dry chalk lands of Picardy and the Somme, with its dry valleys, large fields and a nucleated settlement pattern of many villages but few isolated farms. It was a deformed battlescape that was fought over at least four times before the final British advance in August 1918. This deformed landscape is graphically depicted by Dawson when he writes:

> Our starting point was a little beyond Trônes Wood and a short distance before Angle Wood, after which we were to attack the enemy lines along by Leuze Wood (Lousy Wood) and beyond. The ground over which we had passed and beyond was in a terrible state – villages completely blown away, roads obliterated and unrecognisable, woods blown to pieces only stumps of trees remaining, trenches practically obliterated with shell holes, and other parts consisting of shell holes within shell holes, and hardly a square yard of level ground ... with tangled barbed wire were all over the place.[21]

That advance took them beyond the deformed terrain of the Somme at Bapaume back towards Cambrai and across a battlescape that been fought over and occupied the

19   Simon Peaple, *Mud, Blood and Determination: The History of the 46th (North Midland) Division in the Great War,* (Helion and Company Ltd., Solihull, 2015), p. 127.
20   TNA, WO95/168,SS1226/14, 17 March 1917. Quoted in Senior, Michael, *Haking: A Dutiful Soldier,* (Barnsley, Pen & Sword military, 2012), p. 258.
21   Dawson, *Reminiscences of my Experiences in the First Tanks,* p. 4.

A deformed landscape [Ypres]. (TCMA)

The landscape of Picardy between Albert and Bapaume. (Author)

The landscape of the Pays de Cambresis. (Author)

previous year. It was familiar to Reconnaissance Officers but in 1918 consisted of untended and overgrown fields that concealed debris and forgotten military mine-fields. Here also rivers like the Somme above Peronne and the Selle and the canals (Nord, St. Quentin and Sambre) lay athwart the line of advance.

Beyond the Hindenburg (*Siegfriedstellung*) Line tank routes crossed a pristine land-scape that had not been fought over since 1914. Here lack of maps, undamaged villages and woods that concealed anti-tank weapons presented the Reconnaissance Officers and tank crews with further challenges. Approaching the Belgian border, beyond Le Cateau, was a landscape that more resembled the bocage of Normandy with smaller fields, 'orchards, with 20 feet hedges, and ditches, which afforded excellent cover for the enemy machine guns, rendering them extremely difficult to locate.'[22]

The third variable that challenges a chronological approach is the operational **tactics** in the deployment of the tanks. Once again it is beyond the scope of this account to describe these in any great detail. Tank operations and tactics between 1916 and 1918 showed no simple linear development or 'learning curve.' Broadly they fell into four categories: positional (trench) warfare; all arms warfare; mobile warfare and defensive operations.

---

22   A.H.T. Somers, *The War History of the Sixth Tank Battalion*, (Privately published, 1919, reprinted Naval & Military press), p. 195.

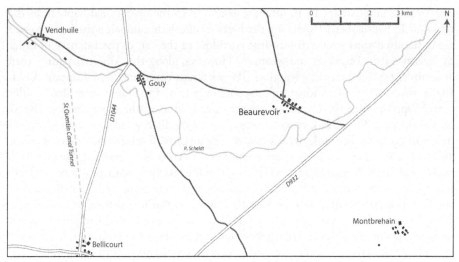

The landscape close to the Hindenburg Line.

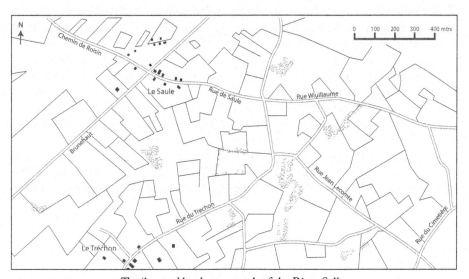

The 'bocage' landscape north of the River Selle.

In positional warfare the tanks were introduced and used as an auxiliary support for the infantry often in small numbers ('penny packets'). Essentially their tactical role was to *break in* to the German defences by crushing barbed wire and destroying machine guns. Colonel E.D. Swinton noted in his paper on the employment of tanks in February 1916 that the tank 'is primarily a machine gun destroyer, which can be employed as an auxiliary to an infantry assault.'[23] In the operational baptism of the tanks on 15 September 1916 during the Flers-Courcelette campaign the tanks passed along hundred yard wide artillery-free corridors in the van of the infantry in order to destroy enemy obstacles and weapons. However, along the Albert-Bapaume road at Courcelette there was an exception. The six tanks, commanded by Captain A. M. Inglis, shadowed the Canadian infantry and only two of the tanks were able to offer useful support when the Canadian infantry was held up at the sugar factory. The 37 tanks utilised in the Flers-Courcelette operation were distributed across ten Divisions in 'penny packets.' The tanks were similarly employed with minimum and local effect, although used in increasingly greater numbers at Arras (60 tanks), at Messines (88 tanks) and Third Ypres, (180 tanks). This role in the relatively static positional warfare was their essential *raison d'etre* and goes some way to explain their employment in small sections rather than as a concentrated force. At this initial stage of tank opera- tions the new weapon was regarded by GHQ as supplementary to the infantry and not an independent arm. Hence tank operations had to adjust to infantry tactics instead of those tactics taking cognizance of the technical limitations of the early tanks and adapting their plans appropriately.[24] This would not occur before the Cambrai opera- tion a year later.

The all arms operations was introduced at Cambrai on 20 November 1917 (378 fighting tanks and 98 support tanks) and then the local battle of Hamel, 4 July 1918 (60 tanks including the new Mark V) and the Battle of Amiens, 8-12 August 1918 (430 tanks including the Medium ['Whippet'] tanks). Here the tanks operated in the larger numbers that the Tank Corps HQ had long wished. However, in the event, they suffered considerable wastage.[25] The tactics now included increased cooperation and mutual support with infantry, artillery and aircraft and all to great effect.[26] The tanks were now in a position to *break-through* enemy defences. Liaison with these other arms was now an essential task for the Intelligence and Reconnaissance Officers.

The third tactical use for tanks, the *break-out* or pursuit, during the 'Hundred Days' that followed the success at the Battle of Amiens, never seriously occurred. The limited tactical operations of the tanks during the 'Hundred Day' are a major source

23   E.D. Swinton, 'Notes on the Employment of Tanks' (1919) quoted in Pidgeon, *Tanks at Flers*, p. 222.

24   For example, the disastrous decision of Lieutenant General Sir William Pulteney to insist that the tank attack on 15 September 1916 in support of the 47th (London) Division should penetrate High Wood against the advice of both Swinton in his aforementioned notes and Elles. Indeed, the former wrote that 'woods and closely planted orchards (also) form an absolute obstacle to their movement.'

25   By day two of the Amiens offensive 155 tanks were in action; on day three only 85 tanks were employed and on day four there were 38 tanks in action. Williams-Ellises, *The Tank Corps*, pp. 193-211. On day two at Cambrai only 52.2% of the tanks were available.

26   Hammond, *Theory and Practice of Tank Cooperation with other Arms on the Western Front during the First World War.*

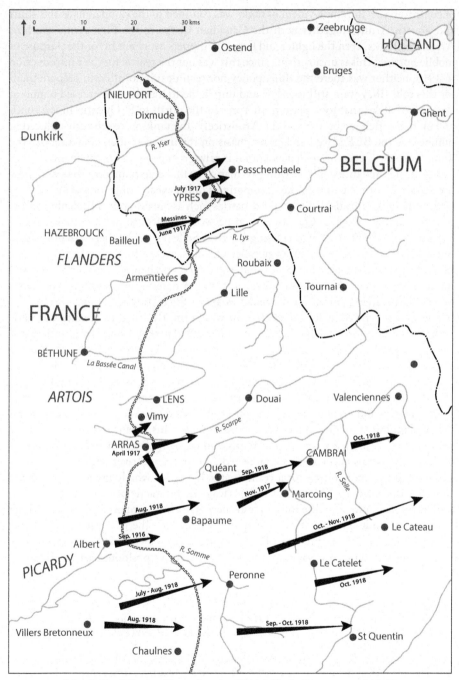

Map 2 The Western Front showing British Tank Operations 1916-18.

of controversy.[27] The employment of tanks was confined to the campaigns of the Third and Fourth Armies together with the Canadian Corps of the First Army south of Arras. The tanks, even the lighter and faster 'Whippets' were not fit for the purpose of mobile pursuit. This is unsurprising since this was not the reason for their introduction in 1916, neither was there the time, policy nor technical innovation to prepare them for this role. They were still too slow and unreliable to match the increased tempo of successive battles that took place from Ypres in the north to St Quentin in the south and on to the Belgian border and the Armistice.[28] The tanks were seriously reduced in numbers as the BEF placed greater emphasis on the use of artillery and aircraft. The Tank Corps was even more dependent on it salvage, repairs and maintenance activities at its maintenance depot at Erin (see map 5) to make up numbers. They were now used again in either 'penny packets', sometimes only two at a time, or assembled in as larger numbers as available for set piece battles such as breaking the Hindenburg Line over the tunnel of the St Quentin Canal between Bellicourt and Vendouille on 27 September 1918 (175 tanks) or crossing the river Selle on 17 October 1918 (48 tanks). The ROs, in spite of the reduced number of tanks, were often stretched as actions moved on rapidly before they could undertake a comprehensive reconnaissance and intelligence appreciation. Reconnaissance Officers determined the necessary post-operational 'rallying points' for the tanks whatever the tactical situation.

The fourth type of major tank action in which the ROs had to operate was altogether different. On 21 March 1918 the Germans launched their long anticipated Spring Offensive, a series of battles they called the *Kaiserschlacht* (the Emperor's Battle). Tank Corps Intelligence and Reconnaissance Officers had two principal tasks between January 1918 and the opening of the German offensive. It was anticipated that the enemy would use tanks in the attack. It was necessary, therefore, to determine numbers and prepare counter measures. A second task was to undertake contingency planning through 'protective reconnaissance.' This meant reconnoitring areas behind the British lines where British tanks could take up defensive positions. Further back supply dumps needed to be established and routes and river crossings prepared. Positions were reconnoitred for a counter attack role for which again they were not fitted for this purpose. This included the 'savage rabbit' tactic of which Fuller was so critical (see Chapter 13). The initial rapid success of the Germans against the British Fifth Army rendered many of these preparations invalid. The ROs then found themselves either operating as infantry officers commanding Lewis Gun teams made up of their 'unhorsed' tank crews or preparing further defensive positions particularly south of Arras.

27   Travers, Tim, 'Could the Tanks of 1918 Have Been War winners for the British Expeditionary Force?', *Journal of Contemporary History,* Vol. 27, (1992), pp. 389-406) and Harris, J.P., *Men, Ideas and Tanks.*
28   Peter Simkins, 'Somme Reprise: Reflections on the Fighting for Albert and Bapaume, August 1918 in Brian Bond et al., *Look to Your Front,* (Staplehurst, Spellmount, 1999), p. 156.

The fourth imperative that the ROs had to consider in undertaking operations was the **Training** of tank and unit commanders for the battle ahead. This will be considered in detail in Chapter 9.

Before launching into a detailed consideration of Tank Corps intelligence and reconnaissance operations bearing in mind these four **T**s it will be necessary to clarify the four key concepts included in the title of this account: 'Reconography', 'Tank Corps' and 'Intelligence and Reconnaissance'.

3

Reconography, Intelligence & Reconnaissance

'Reconnaissance' and 'Intelligence' are terms that are often used interchangeably although Intelligence has wider implications for information gathering as James Beach has shown.[1] In the context of the Tank Corps itself the distinctions were as much administrative as operational. 'Intelligence Officer' (IO) was the title the War Office reserved for the 'General Staff Officer 2 (Intelligence)' (GSO2 I) and Tank Brigade (Reconnaissance) Officers. Both were ranked as majors or above. Battalion and Company 'Intelligence Officers' were designated 'Reconnaissance Officers' (ROs) and were respectively captains or subalterns.[2] For convenience all ranks will be referred to as Reconnaissance Officers (ROs) since their responsibilities differed in degree rather than in kind. Beach concurs when he writes that 'the work of the IOs and ROs ... was an accidental hybrid organisation that, from the start, had to fuse intelligence and reconnaissance practices ... Therefore the use of "reconnaissance" as an umbrella term for all information gathering was logical if potentially confusing to a modern reader.'[3] An alternative 'umbrella term' used in this account which avoids confusing the terms 'reconnaissance' and 'intelligence' yet combines both concepts together with other responsibilities is 'Reconography' (see below).

The conventional term 'Reconnaissance' will be employed here to cover both first hand *primary* information gathering activities by visual means and *secondary* activities, that is, information gathered through second-hand or vicarious sources, for example, maps, air photographs ('Image Intelligence' or Iint), unit reports, prisoner interrogations and interviews with refugees ('Human Intelligence' or Humint).[4] Together

---

1   James Beach, 'British Intelligence and the German Army, 1914-1918', (PhD thesis, University College, London, 2004).
2   WO158/836, 'Military Headquarters, Correspondence and Papers 1 September 1916-31 October 1916', 20 October 1916.
3   James Beach, 'Scouting for Brigands: British Tank Corps Reconnaissance and Intelligence, 1916-18 in Searle (ed), *Genesis, Employment and Aftermath*, p. 111
4   Whilst the reader may be more used to the term 'reconnaissance' being applied only to 'field work', the present writer learned as an undergraduate in Historical Geography that

both primary and secondary reconnaissance today would be designated as 'Geospatial Intelligence' (Geoint). Reconnaissance operations included 'spying out' both any allied territory tanks had to cross, no man's land and where possible enemy territory, what Mitchell described as 'the art of spying out the enemy's land.'[5] However, in this monograph, the term 'Intelligence' will be confined to what Mitchell called 'planning.' This was a *process* that included the higher order cognitive work of the collation, analysis and evaluation of information gathered and its communication through skilful, usually graphical, representations. Hence 'Reconography' is here employed as a collective term that includes Intelligence, Reconnaissance and graphical activities. The terms 'Intelligence' and 'Reconnaissance', however, will continue to be used throughout this work since they are well known whilst 'Reconography' is not established in the military lexicon. Whilst these were the principal tasks of the ROs it will become evident that their roles as Reconographers included other related activities. (fig.1). Reconographic activities are summed up by J.F.C. Fuller when he noted that

> in turn must each move or preparatory measure be dealt with, reconnaissance playing an all important part, not only before the battle, but during it, and immediately after it, and if the system of communication during the battle is not efficient the work of the reconnaissance officer will frequently be wasted, so we find one preparation depending for its worth on another until the whole forms a complete and somewhat intricate chain.[6]

At the outset it is also essential to recognise that reconnaissance was not solely the responsibility of the ROs. Both tank unit commanders and tank commanders were expected through Standing Orders to undertake their own visual reconnaissance albeit guided by their unit ROs

Reconnaissance is a fundamental military skill undertaken by all arms. Intelligence and Reconnaissance has a long and distinguished pedigree. Von Clausewitz refers to 'information' in which 'we denote all the knowledge which we have of the enemy and his country; therefore, in fact, the foundation of all our ideas and actions.'[7] It is a critical operation carried out prior to military engagements and has been employed since the advent of armies. The principles behind tank reconnaissance can, therefore, be traced back at least to Von Clausewitz if not Sun Tzu.[8] The introduction of the tank on the Western Front on 15 September 1916 and later actions on the Somme during the autumn included reconnaissance as a matter of course. Brigadier

---

'field work' could also take place in the 'muniment room' where knowledge is acquired through the 'finger tips' as well as in the field and through the soles of one's boots.

5   Mitchell, *Tank Warfare*, p. 307.
6   Fuller, *Tanks in the Great War*, p.106.
7   Clausewitz, *On War, Book One, Chapter VI* M. Howard & P. Paret, eds. (Princeton University Press, 1992).
8   Sun Tzu, *The Art of War* (Pax Librorum Publishing House, trans. Lionel Giles, 2009).

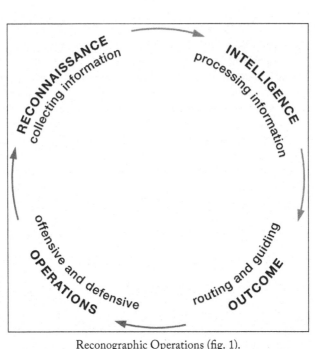

Reconographic Operations (fig. 1).

B.A.H. Parritt places reconnaissance in its historical context.[9] The first decade of the twentieth century and particularly the Boer War brought reconnaissance into greater prominence.[10] The three seminal works published before 1914, which should have provided the template for the reconnaissance operations of the first tanks, were *Field Service Regulations, Part I, (Operations)*[11] together with Brigadier David Henderson's *The Art of Reconnaissance*[12] and Baden Powell's *Aids to Scouting for NCOs and Men*. The latter is perhaps more relevant for reconnaissance in Imperial environments rather than European. David Henderson's work is virtually a text book on the subject. The South African War gave special emphasis to reconnaissance. Spencer Jones opines that 'throughout the Edwardian period reconnaissance was seen as a crucial duty'[13] yet he also identifies the weakness to which the first tank commanders became heir

9   B. A. H. Parritt, *The Intelligencers* (Barnsley, Pen & Sword Military, 2011).
10   G. F. R., Henderson, *The Science of War: A Collection of Essays And Lectures 1891-1903* (London, Longmans, Green, and Co., 1912 [1905]), p. 372. S. Jones, *From Boer War to World War: Tactical reform of the British Army, 1902-1914* (Norman, University of Oklahoma Press, 2012), p. 201.
11   War Office, *Field Service Regulations, Part I, Operations 1909, reprinted with amendments 1912* (London, HMSO, 1912).
12   D. Henderson, *The Art of Reconnaissance* (London, John Murray, 1915 [1907].
13   Jones, *From Boer War to World War*, p. 201

Brigadier David Henderson.
(Open source)

when he wrote that 'practical training in scouting against active opposition (was) to become neglected.'[14] Lord Roberts' Director of Intelligence and distinguished former Staff College lecturer, Colonel G.F.R. Henderson, recognized that 'Reconnaissance, even more important than heretofore, is far more difficult.'[15]

David Henderson's book also has its origins in the South African War when he wrote *Field Intelligence: Its Principals and Practice*.[16] Brigadier Henderson was commissioned in the Argyll and Sutherland Highlanders before graduating in 1896 from the Staff College.[17] He served as Kitchener's Director of Military Intelligence in the Boer war and was caught up in the siege of Ladysmith 'when he provided successful reconnaissance support and leadership during a raid against Boer guns.'[18] He was awarded the DSO in 1902. 'Henderson's writings on intelligence and reconnaissance demonstrated his cautious approach to progress and reform ... (he) recognised the growing

14   Ibid., p. 197.
15   G. F. R.Henderson, *The Science of War–A Collection of Essays And Lectures 1891-1903*, p. 372.
16   D. Henderson, *Field Intelligence: Its Principles and Practice*, (London, HMSO, 1904).
17   J. Pugh, 'David Henderson and Command of the Royal Flying Corps' in *Stemming the Tide, Officers and Leadership in the British Expeditionary Force 1914* (Wolverhampton Military Studies No. 1, Solihull, Helion & Co. Ltd, 2013) pp. 267-268.
18   Ibid., p.269.

importance of technological solutions to the challenges facing military professionals.'[19] One of his technological solutions was aviation in which he became an authority. In the later editions of *The Art of Reconnaissance* he referred to the importance of aerial reconnaissance. These views, together with the support of Field Marshal Sir John French, led to his appointment to command of the Royal Flying Corps with the British Expeditionary Force (BEF) in 1914.

In *The Art of Reconnaissance* arguably his definition of reconnaissance was too narrow when he confined it to 'personal observation' alone.[20] He also dismissed 'topography' as 'the favourite field of the military pedant that has acquired an exaggerated impor-tance.' Not gifted with second sight, he could not visualize the importance of this topic for tank operations.[21] He was also unhappy with the distinction between strategic and tactical reconnaissance although they are useful concepts in Tank Corps reconnais-sance operations.[22] Two of his three types of reconnaissance were particularly perti-nent to future Tank RO's activities. His 'independent system' was that undertaken by patrols and scouting parties. Their discretion was wide and range unlimited. They sought to obtain their information without being observed and were not intended to fight but to elude the enemy.[23] A second type which became important in the first few months of 1918 was 'protective reconnaissance' which 'is used for purposes of security or of protection or of both.'[24] His third type, 'contact reconnaissance', was less relevant to Tank ROs since it was 'that employed by large bodies, which seek out the enemy and are prepared to fight, if necessary, for the information they desire.'[25] There is a case to be made for this form of reconnaissance in the last weeks of the war with the employment of 17th (Armoured Car) Battalion, 3rd Tank Brigade.[26] Future tank ROs would recognise the techniques he proposed for effective reconnaissance. David Henderson's view that 'the wider the knowledge of the informant, the more useful the information' would also be adopted by senior tank Intelligence Officers.[27] It is difficult to imagine that the authors of *FSR Part I* were not influenced by this earlier book since there is considerable overlap between the two works.

'Time spent on reconnaissance is seldom wasted' has almost become a mantra.[28] The sections of *FSR Part1* relevant to reconnaissance should have provided the tenets

19   Ibid., p. 270.
20   D. Henderson, *The Art of Reconnaissance*, p.9.
21   Ibid., pp. 148-149.
22   Ibid., p. 21.
23   Ibid., p. 11.
24   Ibid.,10.
25   Ibid.,11.
26   TNA, WO95/105, 3rd Tank Brigade HQ January 1918 to 1919.
27   Ibid., p. 148.
28   War Office, *Field Service Regulations, Part I,, Operations, reprinted with amendments 1912* (London, HMSO, 1912), p.117.

for the first tanks.[29] The precepts of reconnaissance set out in *FSR Part1* can be traced in tank reconnaissance training in 1918.[30] *FSR Part1* made it clear that although the principles and skills of reconnaissance 'has been considered chiefly from the point of view of the cavalry, it is equally the duty of infantry.'[31] If the authors had also been gifted with foresight they might have added 'and tanks.' *FSR Part I* even warned that Standing Orders 'unless carefully revised and kept up to date ... may lead to misunderstandings.'[32]

Much of what is included in 'Chapter VII: Information' of *FSR Part I* resonates with later operations of the tank ROs, in particular the definition of directed or 'tactical reconnaissance.' Here 'information may be obtained –

i.   By personal observation on the part of the commander
ii.   By general staff or other officers, patrols or scouts
iii. By the air service'[33]

The section on exploratory or 'Strategic Reconnaissance' is also relevant as demonstrated later in the case of Arras, Third Ypres and Cambrai. They afforded 'the Commander-in-Chief with information on which to base his strategical (sic) plan of operation.'[34] Protective Reconnaissance, noted above, became important in the winter and spring 1918.[35] There are also sections (97 and 98) referring to 'Reconnaissance during battle' and 'Transmission of information' that became central to the reconographic role of the ROs.[36] *FSR Part 1* also offers pointers to the selection of ROs who 'must be highly trained, have considerable technical knowledge, be quick and intelligent observers, be possessed of judgement and determination' operating with the best equipment.[37] The *Field Service Regulations* promoted the principle that reconnaissance troops 'must not be unduly restricted in their movements' thereby encouraging their independent mobility.[38] This provided the ROs with a licence to roam with the aid of vehicles especially motor cycles. It gave them an independence that other Tank Corps personnel did not have. Since the tanks needed 'to avoid observation, particularly when the enemy is provided with aircraft' Chapter IX, 'Night Operations', is especially

29 Hammond, 'The Theory and Practice of Tank Cooperation with other Arms on the Western Front during the First World War', (Abstract) shows how FSR 1 provided a framework for all tank operations.
30 TNA, WO95/118, '6th Brigade Training Centre, 01 January1917-30 December 1918', indicates the principles behind reconnaissance training.
31 *FSR I*, p. 116.
32 Ibid., p. 26.
33 Ibid., pp.116-118.
34 Ibid., pp. 114-115.
35 Ibid., pp. 123-124.
36 Ibid., p. 124.
37 Ibid., p. 117.
38 Ibid., p. 113.

relevant.[39] Night marches depend upon 'the care and thoroughness, and particularly on the completeness of the preliminary Reconnaissance' on which 'the success of the night operations, next to the special training of troops to work in the darkness, chiefly depends.'[40] 'Preparation for Night Advances and Night Assaults' has much that is relevant to tank movements but was neglected prior to the first tank operation on 15 September 1916.[41] Before the Battle of Flers-Courcelette the first tanks also procured 'local guides', as *FSR Part I* advised.[42] The infantry guides, however, created more problems for the tank commanders than they solved.

In 1920 Hodder & Stoughton published on behalf of *The Pelman Institute* a slim volume, 56 pages long. It was entitled *Reconography-Simplified Reconnaissance Sketching.* The author was 'GRAPHITE', a 'Pelman Student in the B.E.F.' Pelmanism was concerned with memory training. The content was based upon instruction given during the Great War in 1917-18 to Reconnaissance Officers in training.[43] *Graphite* states that a purpose of Reconography 'is to give them (tank commanders) all the information that they want, or ought to want, and ought to have. All about ... objectives, obstacles, defences, landmarks, targets and routes.'[44]

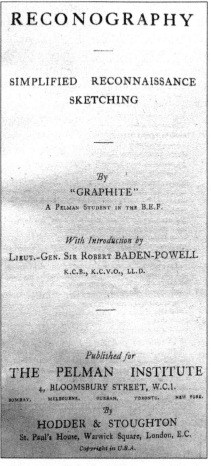

The cover of the booklet *Reconography*.
(TCWEF)

The body of the booklet with its many illustrations aims to demonstrate the simplicity of field sketching. *Graphite* defines the essentials of the task as: **T**ime to

---

39   Ibid., p. 177.
40   Ibid., p. 176.
41   Ibid., pp. 184-187.
42   Ibid., p. 179.
43   The author claimed not to have retained a copy. There are at least three duplicates in the United Kingdom at the Bodleian Library, British Library and Imperial War Museum.
44   Graphite, *Reconography, Simplified Reconnaissance Sketching* (Hodder & Stoughton, 1920), p.7.

be of use; **R**elevancy to the object; **A**ccuracy as circumstances permit and 'what went ye out for to see' and **C**larity, clear and legible. He encapsulates these in the acronym **TRAC**.

'The Aim of a Military Sketch should be to convey certain information in a form so concise and precise, that the gist of the matter instantly leaps to the eye without the slightest ambiguity.' The field sketch is described as a 'reconogram' since 'it is really comparable to a telegram sent by a very poor man to a very stupid man.'[45] The reconogram should include notes as to the subject, purpose and from where it was sketched together with visibility, date and time and authorship (name, rank and unit).

Facetiously he concludes that 'any sketch deficient in its identity disk should be crimed on sight as "idle and improperly dressed".'[46]

A model Reconogram.

Methods demand that 'Intelligent selection is more important than the mere drawing.'[47] Draughtsmanship was discussed in detail. He warned that 'artistic temperament must be ruthlessly suppressed' but he emphasised 'LOOK-THINK-SELECT-DRAW.'[48] He detailed the principal 'Stock Properties' of the landscape under the headings of 'The Works of God'(trees) and 'The Works of Man'(buildings especially churches) (see image 15). Panoramas, with 'a little exaggeration in the vertical scale is permissible and indeed often desirable.'[49] He also discussed 'Memory and Lightening Sketching.' The final sections go beyond just field sketching to include further

45   Ibid, p.12.
46   Ibid, p.13.
47   Ibid, p.18.
48   Ibid, p.19.
49   Ibid, p.46.

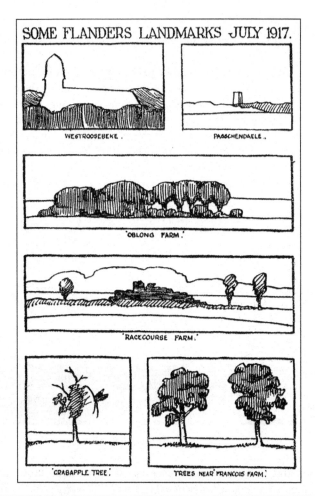

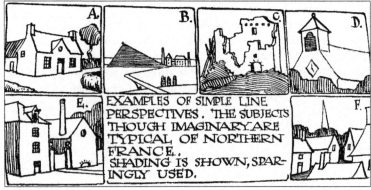

'The Works of God and the Works of Man'.

A Model Panorama. (TCWEF)

graphical representations of the landscape through profile sections and the 'translation of LANDSCAPE into terms of COUNTRY.'[50] This warrants the application of 'Graphite's' neologism, *RECONOGRAPHY*, to three of the principal tasks required of the Reconnaissance Officer: that of information gathering through Reconnaissance together with the selection(Intelligence process) and graphical representation of both the acquired information and the 'battlescape' itself.

The booklet included two further points of interest. The 'Introduction' was written by Lieutenant General Sir Robert Baden Powell, KCB, KCVO, LLD who it has been noted had written his own seminal treaty on reconnaissance whilst at Mafeking.[51] Apparently, he was able to send out a copy before the siege developed. This illustrates the continuity in the importance of reconnaissance work at least as far back as the South African War. It provides further support to Dr Spencer Jones' views on the relevance of the Boer War to operations in the Great War.[52] Baden Powell used the term 'Hierography' rather than 'Reconography.' He considered that 'few even among the soldiers themselves realise the part that small individual enterprises played … Their success was in many cases due to their powers of observation and of recording the things observed.'[53] He also saw it as a life skill 'which, when once acquired, will not only help you as a soldier but will come in with an equal value in almost any line of life'; hence his 'Scouting for Boys.'

In his Preface *Graphite* 'makes so bold as to offer a little advice on lecture room tactics.' This hinted at another important role of the RO which will be considered later, that of training. He also quoted William James in his 'Papers on Philosophy' on the subject of lecturing. Anyone addressing the public whether adults or children, would benefit from the advice proffered here by *Graphite*.

50   Ibid, pp. 53-55.
51   R. Baden-Powell, *Aids to Scouting for NCOs and Men* (1899).
52   S. Jones, 'Scouting for Soldiers, Reconnaissance in the British Cavalry 1899-1914', *War in History*, 18(4), 2011, pp. 495-513 and *From Boer War to World War* (University of Oklahoma Press, 2012).
53   Ibid, p. 2.

Church Steeples near Cambrai. (TCWEF)

The internal evidence of the booklet, especially the illustrations is a clue to the identity of the author. Both the details of the spires of eight churches around Cambrai and the skilled pencil work suggest someone with an architectural background. In his autobiography, *Architect Errant,* Sir Clough Williams-Ellis (formerly Major) admits to the authorship and the pen name *Graphite*.[54] (see below) In the post war world Williams-Ellis was better known as the creator of the Italianate village of Portmeirion, North Wales.

Williams-Ellis volunteered for the army in 1914 at the age of 21. After a failed attempt to join the Household Cavalry he was 'gazetted to that elegant and gallant regiment', the 9th Lancers.[55] He soon transferred to the Imperial Light Horse (ILH) and was made a lieutenant. However the ILH was immediately disbanded so he became an infantry officer in 'a raggle-taggle outfit' belonging to the Royal Fusiliers. Following a course at Chelsea Barracks under Guard Instructors and, 'having savoured the assured professionalism of the Guards, their discipline and apparent efficiency' he then transferred to the newly established Welsh Guards. Shortly after his marriage to Amabel Strachey he was in France in a draft consequent on the large number of Guards' casualties during the Battle of Loos in September 1915. There he found that 'no tedium so utterly blisterings [sic] as that of routine trench warfare in a relatively quiet sector ... and so go off exploring the back areas with a Baedeker, a sketch book and a map.'[56] A consequence was that he became a Guards Intelligence officer (a 'trench rat') and 'in that capacity my map reading, sketching, reconnoitring and reporting propensities could all be employed, and with few routine duties and a general roving commission ... contrived to lead a more useful and less

54   C. Williams-Ellis, *Architect Errant* (London, Constable & Co. 1971), p. 125.
55   Ibid, p. 109.
56   Ibid, pp. 115-116.

devastated existence.'[57] This was useful experience together with balloon and aeroplane reconnaissance which he undertook when he eventually transferred to the Tank Corps.

It was during a second posting to the Ypres salient as Corps GSO3 (Intelligence) that presciently he recognized:

> Someday someone would have to storm the High Command Redoubt that so insolently dominated our front line [the Pilkem Ridge] and if successful, to pass beyond it down into the Steenbeke valley, and with luck up and over the next rise and away beyond. So a 'Book of Beyond must be compiled, from observations, from the deposition of refugees, from maps and photographs and every other imaginable source, and thus might the Intelligence department justify its tedious hibernation in a static warfare sector, and so perhaps be kept usefully amused and out of mischief … had I known that a year later I

The Marriage of Clough Williams-Ellis to Amabel Strachey: this is believed to be the only remaining photograph of Williams-Ellis in uniform. (CWEF)

should find myself … creeping furtively up the Steenbeke itself reconnoitring for likely crossing places, my interest in this mostly invisible enemy hinterland might have been less perfunctory[58] (see below)

He did not endear himself to his commanders by adding facetious and satirical comments to his official daily 'Intelligence Summaries.' The fertile, creative mind and the boredom experienced by this somewhat eccentric intelligence officer encouraged him to devise mantraps to capture the enemy and drag them into the trenches. They were never used. Whilst on a reconnaissance course he had a bout of influenza and during convalescent at St. Pol he paid an unannounced visit to the nearby new Tank HQ at Bermicourt. After an invitation to tea and buttered toast with the Commanding Officer (CO) of the Tank Corps, Lieutenant Colonel (later Major General) H.J. Elles, whom he declared to be a 'fine soldier and leader, there was something engagingly unmilitary about the commander of the tanks', Williams-Ellis 'put in for a Tank Section' and was transferred to the Tank Corps. However, he never commanded a Tank Section, he simply continued as a Reconnaissance and Intelligence Officer in

57   Ibid, pp. 116-117.
58   Ibid, p.122.

the Tanks.[59] At Arras he was the 1st Tank Battalion's R.O. His Commanding Officer was Lieutenant Colonel (later Brigadier) Christopher Baker-Carr. By the Third Ypres Williams-Ellis had become The 1st Tank Brigade's Intelligence Officer and a major. 'But as usual in warfare there was a long, tedious and undramatic wait, during which I tried to work out reconnaissance methods suitable to this new arm.'[60]

One result was the little grey book, *Reconography*, employing Pelman memory training to enable

> Memorizing of landscapes, buildings, trees, trenches and the rest of our battle-scarred scenery, where observation could often be but brief and furtive and immediate sketching quite impossible. So I set to work and showed how almost anyone could, by a simplified quasi-shorthand method, produce a perfectly legible and understandable record of what he had seen, and I drew lots of little pictures in simple outline to show how readily this could be done. There was a section too on 'Reports' and how to make such as short, clear, and unambiguous as possible.[61]

Perhaps his expectations were somewhat ingenuous. In spite of getting Baden-Powell to write the introduction and receiving a fee of £100 the proofs fell foul of the Censors and the booklet was not published until after the war.

It was on 19 August 1917 that Clough Williams-Ellis arguably made a minor but successful contribution to the Third Ypres campaign but perhaps had an even greater importance for the Tank Corps. There is some suggestion that he approached his CO with an unusual idea at that time to capture four German concrete reinforced strong points or MEBUS. These were the reinforced Hillock, Maison de Hibou, Triangle and Cockroft farms and gun pits astride the St Julien – Poelcappelle road (see map 3) He believed this idea might save up to a thousand infantry lives.[62]

Baker-Carr took the idea to the XVIII Corps' commander, Lieutenant General Sir Ivor Maxse. This attentive general officer approved of the idea in spite of the scepticism of his divisional and brigade commanders. The successful 'Cockroft Operation', under the command of Major R. Broome, was born. The MEBUs and gun pits were captured or destroyed and only fifteen infantrymen were wounded instead of an anticipated thousand. It cost the life of one tank commander and two other ranks (ORs). Two further consequences are worthy of note: the tank tactics he recommended heralded those used later at Cambrai (surprise, movement on firm surfaces, no preliminary barrage except the use of smoke, infantry to consolidate after the tanks captured the strong points and even fascines were used to cross the marshy Steenbeek). It also

59   Ibid, p.125.
60   Ibid, p.125.
61   Ibid, pp. 125-126.
62   D. G. Browne, *The Tank in Action During the First World War* (Edinburgh, Blackwood & Sons, 1920), pp.192-240.

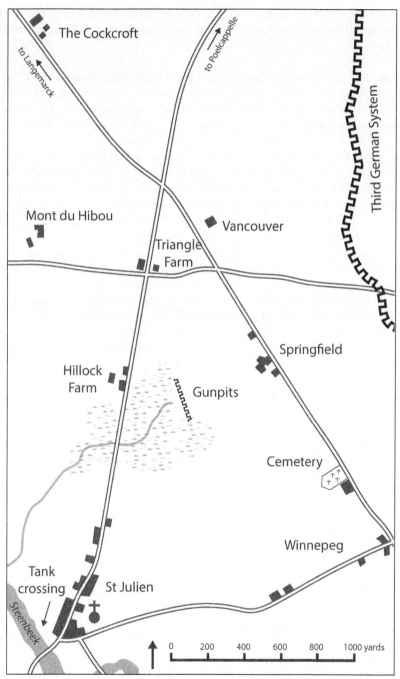

Map 3 Sketch map of the Cockroft Operation.

curbed the opposition of senior officers to the use of tanks which might have led to their decommissioning. Another RO laid an ingenuous claim to this success when he wrote that

> ... we had one success in which I hope I had a hand. Major Broome and I had been talking about the stupidity of putting Tanks into bogs. We agreed that the only possible way was to use what remained of the roads, regardless of the risk of incurring shell fire ... his action became the model for the battle of Cambrai.[63]

In early 1918, Major C. William-Ellis deputised for the GSO2 (I) of the Tank Corps when the latter was absent. Indeed in the last month of the war he replaced him when the GSO2 (I) was severely wounded. Modestly he recalled that 'I found myself promoted to fill as best I might the place he had invested with almost legendary gallantry ... Before I made any blunders ... the Armistice was rumoured and then finally announced.'[64]

Over time and in different environments reconnaissance officers have had different titles: in India they were Guides whilst particularly courageous Indians were employed as 'Pundits' to map the mountainous regions of Central Asia during 'the Great Game'; in South Africa they were Scouts. During the Great War they were officially Reconnaissance Officers and now unofficially Reconographers. In recent times reconnaissance work has been designated as Geospatial Intelligence (Geoint).[65] With such a heritage there seems little excuse for the neglect of reconnaissance skills when tanks were first employed on 15 September 1916.

---

63   N. M. Dillon, 'Record of N. M. Dillon', Special Collection, Brotherton Library, University of Leeds, p. 18.
64   Williams-Ellis, *Architect Errant*, p. 128.
65   U.S. Joint Chiefs of Staff, 2-0, *Joint Intelligence*, Joint Publication 2-0 (Washington D.C. June 22, 2007).

4

In the Beginning

At Dover in early March 1916, Second Lieutenant Basil Lucas Quixano Henriques, a future Company and Battalion Tank Corps Reconnaissance Officer, and his close friend Second Lieutenant George Macpherson were detailed to meet with their Commanding Officer, Lieutenant Colonel H. D. Hurst, of the 3rd East Kent Regiment. This was a holding battalion. At the meeting they were told that he had specially chosen them to be interviewed at the War Office for a mission about which he was very vague. Consequently they were interviewed at the War Office by Colonel E. H. Swinton who was responsible for establishing a 'profoundly new secret unit of the Machine Gun Corps'. Henrique's description of their interview suggests that it was perfunctory in the extreme. It explored neither the reason for their attendance nor their qualifications for the 'mission'. Indeed Henriques seemed quite wrong for the task ahead. He was totally 'unmechanical', could not drive, had never used a Lewis gun and at 6'3" would have great difficulty squeezing into confined spaces. At least Macpherson could drive. They were to join the heavy section of the Motor Machine Gun Corps (MMGC) at Aldershot. Colonel Swinton made it clear that if these disadvantages proved too much they would quickly be 'RTUed' (Returned To Unit) within a fortnight.[1]

Basil Henriques was born on the 17 October, 1890 at 17, Sussex Square, London. He was the youngest son of a wealthy Jewish Sephardim family. His three older brothers all served in the Great War. The eldest, Julian, was a Company commander in the 1st Battalion, Queen's Westminster Rifles (16th Brigade, 56th London Division). This was a Territorial unit. He became second in command of the Battalion and later, having survived the war, wrote the history of the unit.[2] His second brother Ronald was a regular officer in the Royal West Surrey Regiment. He was killed at Paisy

---

1   B. L. Q. Henriques, *Indiscretions of a Warden* (London, Methuen & Co. Ltd., 1937), pp 112-113.
2   J.Q. Henriques, *The War History of the 1st Battalion Queen's Westminster Rifles 1914-1918* (London, Medici Society Ltd., 1923).

on the Aisne on 14 September 1914. The third brother, Harold, volunteered for the Household cavalry and saw service in the Ypres salient.

Henriques' civil career had taken a radically different route from that of his brothers' business activities. He described his occupation on his army attestation form as 'Social Worker'. Henriques went up to Oxford in 1910. In his second year he met the person he described as 'the greatest inspiration in my life', Alec Pattison. He read his book, *Across the Bridges* which depicted the squalor of the slums in Bermondsey and the need for people to take positive action to improve life there. A further lifelong influence was Claude Montefiore a leading proponent of 'Liberal Judaism'. He had learned from his mother that Judaism and English culture were mutually enriching. During the vacations whilst at Oxford Henriques undertook mission work in the slums of Bermondsey. It became imperative for him to establish a permanent mission for poor Jewish families in the East End of London. Five months before the outbreak of the First World War he achieved his ambition and opened the 'Oxford and St. George's Jewish Lads' Club' on 3 March, 1914 at Betts Street, Stepney in the East End of London. Furthermore he felt compelled to leave the palatial West End and live 'over the shop' at Betts St. He believed that religion must be the inspiration of social justice.[3] He also felt that those privileged in society had to 'join hands with the under-privileged' to achieve social justice and that they had 'to care for each other, suffer with each other and feel themselves at one with each other'.

By 1915 he considered the Settlement was sufficiently well established under the watchful eye of his co-worker Rose Loewe that he felt confident enough in the new club to volunteer for the army. The following year he married Rose but it was an unconsummated marriage but a successful partnership. He was commissioned in November 1915 in the East Kent Regiment although he had hoped to follow Ronald into the West Surreys. After a period in an Officer Training Unit back at Oxford he was posted to Dover.

At Dover he met nineteen year old George Macpherson who had left Winchester in July 1915 and who had begun the process of applying for an appointment to the special reserve of officers. On 22 August Macpherson was certified fit for military service and was recommended to the War Office by the Commanding Officer of the 3rd Buffs. The date he was commissioned in the Buffs, 15th September 1915, became a fateful date and was a month before Basil enlisted.

At Dover they soon discovered one another and a close relationship developed between the older and formidable Henriques and this younger attractive man. Henriques describes George Macpherson as 'tall, with an almost girlish complexion and pure light blue eyes'.[4] This description bears 'all the hallmarks of the English

3   Henriques, *Indiscretions of a Warden.*
4   Henriques, *Indiscretions of a Warden*, p. 112.

Lieutenant Basil Henriques 1916. (TCMA)   Lieutenant George Macpherson. (WCA)

public school homo-eroticism'.[5] In many ways they were so different. They were separated by at least six years in age. One was a Sephardic Jew the other a devoted Anglican Christian. However these differences did not conceal far more profound qualities which they shared and which drew them together. They recognized in each other a simple but profound religious faith in a shared God which they believed motivated all their actions. Macpherson was probably attracted by Henriques' work in the East End and was inspired to undertake something similar in the urban slums.[6] He communicated to his family that 'he was dreaming of a life spent in the slums of our great cities rescuing those that are ready to perish'.[7]

On 14th March, 1916 they took the train together to Brookwood Station, Aldershot and to Bisley

> only to be told that the ever mysterious Motor Machine Gun Corps had left two days before for Siberia. Tableau! Siberia, however, proved to be a camp not so far from Bisley as to be beyond the radius of the station cab in which they both presently set off.[8]

On arrival they had an informal lunch with the CO of C Company of the Motor Machine Gun Corps, Major Allen Holford-Walker, formerly of the Argyll and

5   Susan England, 'Three English Jews: Identity, Modernity and the Experience of War', unpublished thesis, University of Southampton.
6   George had already experiences mission work in the slums of Portsmouth whilst at Winchester College.
7   Gutherie, Rev report in *Huntly Express*, 29 September 1916.
8   C. & A Williams Ellis, *The Tank Corps* (Country Life, 1919), p.17.

Sutherland Highlanders. They learned they would have to 'drive an armed caterpillar which could go through and over anything and knock trees down' although Holford-Walker admitted that had not even seen one himself.[9] This was to be the 'tank'. By the time they had reached their Suffolk training area, at the estate of Lord Iveagh at Lodge Farm, Elveden, near Thetford, the unit had already been re-designated in May as the Heavy Section Motor Machine Corps (HSMGC). It was under this title that Henriques, Macpherson and the tanks experienced their baptism of fire on the 15 September 1916.

Henriques' and Macpherson's story now merges with those of the other volunteers. According to Major Allen Holford-Walker the selection of officers was based on whether they came from the Motor Machine Gun Corps; were sent by the War Office as 'mechanical gentlemen', i.e. owners of motor cars and cycles and side cars; were appointed by influence or were obtained by Holford-Walker himself.[10] They were the first men to command a tank in battle with six months training and preparation before going into action: it was preparation that neglected the important skill of reconnaissance. Most of their time now was spent at Lodge Farm, Elveden, Suffolk. The estate was surrounded by guards and the utmost secrecy. It was described as 'a camp more ringed about than was the palace of the Sleeping Beauty, and more zealously guarded than the Paradise of a Shah.'[11] In retrospect Henriques regretted the time wasted on camouflaging the tanks and regarding their training as 'one huge game' where they 'looked for trees to knock down'. He agreed with his company commander, Major Allen Holford-Walker, who was later to complain to General J.F.C. Fuller about the lack of discipline evident amongst the first volunteers. Henriques wrote that they had imagined themselves 'slowly wending our way to Berlin over beautiful parkland such as we were now practising on' but, in fact, their training in the few and shared tanks and across contrived battlefields was no preparation for what lay ahead.[12]

On 25 August 1916, C Company, HSMGC, arrived in France. Henriques and Macpherson, both now promoted to the rank of Lieutenant, and their Section Commander, Captain Bruce Holford-Walker, but always known as Archie (brother of their Company Commander, Allen Halford-Walker), had marched their men across Waterloo Bridge *en route* for the station and France. Henriques' wife Rose was there to record the entraining with her box brownie camera and photographed Henriques and Macpherson at Waterloo Station. They landed at Le Havre and moved on to Rouen, thence by rail to the St. Riquier training area at Yvrench close to Abbeville. Their tanks came via Avonmouth. Henriques' destination was the Somme where he

---

9   Henriques, *Indiscretions of a Warden*, pp.113-114.
10   Letter to General Fuller, National Army Museum, Holford-Walker Papers.
11   Clough William-Ellis & A. William-Ellis, Ibid., pp 18.
12   Henriques, *Indiscretions of a Warden*, p. 114. In fact trenches were dug and shell holes created across which they also drove.

C Company, HSMGC, crossing Waterloo Bridge on the way to France: L. to R. Capt.
Bruce Holford-Walker, Lieut. Macpherson, Lieut. Henriques, Major Allen Holford-Walker.
(TCMA)

Henriques and Macpherson
at Waterloo Station. (HPSU)

saw his first action as a tank commander in the Heavy Section Machine Gun Corps (HSMGC).

On 16 November 1916 the HSMGC was re-designated as the Heavy Branch Machine Gun Corps (HBMGC). It fought under this name at Arras in April 1917 when by this time Henriques had returned to France after re-training as a Reconnaissance Officer, and at Messines in June 1917. It was on 27 July, when it was recognized by Royal Warrant as the Tank Corps (TC) and by this time Henriques had become a Company RO preparing for the Third Ypres.[13] In the following account the present writer follows Douglas Browne' advice that 'for simplicity and common sense I have written throughout of the "Tank Corps" where a pedantic conscience would have impelled me to speak of the H.B.M.G.C.,[and H.S.M.G.C.] for this change of nomenclature with all it implied was not in force until late in 1917'.[14] It is also convenient here to refer to the Tank Units simply as the Tank Corps (TC) rather than use all these earlier titles.

13   Gibot & Gorczynski, *Following the Tanks*, p.37.
14   Browne, *The Tank in Action*, p. 318.

5

Reconnaissance with the First Tanks

> ... this is why we failed – in our knowledge of reconnaissance. We did not know what to look for, and we did not know how to look for it or where to look for it ...[1]

This was the admission of Lieutenant Basil L.Q. Henriques in a lecture he gave to tank officers in training at Bovington on 6 March 1917 following recovery from wounds he received on 15 September 1916. The point he made indicated the gap between the official views about reconnaissance expressed in *FSR I* and the practices of the first tank commanders. It was one of the principal reasons which led later to the establishment of a specially trained group of Intelligence and Reconnaissance Officers. He confessed that as a Tank Commander he was ignorant of the application of *Field Service Regulations* to tank reconnaissance.[2] Though critical of his own preparation for action he was keen to show in the lecture his support for the new Tank Corps' training policies that were then addressing the problem. In March 1917 the policies on training, including reconnaissance, were the responsibility of Brigadier General W. Glasgow at the new Tank Depot, Bovington, Dorset and Major J.F.C. Fuller in Tank HQ, Bermicourt.

On 9 September 1916, Henriques and the majority of the tanks of 'C' and 'D' Companies detrained from St. Riquier at the Bronfay Farm sidings of the 'The Loop' (the 'Plateau line') north of Bray. The event is commemorated by a mural on the wall of the farm. Henriques' tank, number 533, a 'female' with machine guns, was renumbered C22 and Macpherson's (originally 523) C20 (a 'male' tank with 6 pounder guns), while Holford-Walker's originally 705 was now C19. In addition, Holford-Walker's tank was christened 'Clan Leslie' in acknowledgement of his Scottish ancestry. In recognition that they were C Company tanks they were all prefixed with the letter C.

---

1 B. L. Q. Henriques, 'Attack on the Quadrilateral' (a transcription of a lecture with hand written amendments delivered on the 6 March 1917, Tank Corps Museum & Archives) p. 6.
2 Ibid.,, p.15.

Both C and D Companies began to prepare for their contribution to the forth-coming Flers-Courcelette offensive. In his lecture, Lieutenant Henriques gave a detailed account of his reconnaissance activities with two other Tank Commanders in C Company together with their movements between their arrival at 'The Loop' and the attack on 15 September 1916.[3] His own inexperience was underpinned by a fundamental error he admitted to when he wrote: 'I had not realised before that the training of a soldier as laid down in Field Service Regulations and Infantry Training apply equally to the Tank Commander and to a Tank crew.'[4]

The eighteen tanks of C Company commanded by Major Allen Holford-Walker were charged to support the XIV Corps under Lieutenant General the Earl of Cavan. They were the right wing of the British offensive. A further six tanks of C Company were tasked to support the Canadians who were to attacked Courcelette on the left wing of the offensive. Henriques and Macpherson were in Number 4 Section led by Captain Archie Holford-Walker. There were six tanks in the Section but three were placed in Corps' reserve. The plan was that three tanks of 4 Section were to capture the village of Morval passing through the recently captured Quadrilateral redoubt. Major General Ross commanding 6th Division planned to attack with two brigades, the 71st under Brigadier General Fitz. M. Edwards (whose HQ was at Arrowhead Copse south east of Trônes Wood) and the 16th Brigade commanded by Brigadier General W.L. Osborn. His HQ was in the quarry south of Wedge Wood on the Maurepas-Ginchy road.

On the second day at the Bray Plateau, 10 September, Henriques undertook a frus-trating bicycle reconnaissance together with his Section Commander, Captain A. Holford-Walker, and George Macpherson.[5] This proved to be an unsuccessful attempt to meet the first part of Point 3 in 'Instructions for the Employment of "Tanks."' that read 'very careful reconnaissance should be made of routes and positions of departure, and routes marked out by tapes.'[6] 'Our general idea was to get some knowledge of the country in which we were to operate.' It seemed that this was a failure since they had no idea what to look for, where to look or indeed how to make a successful reconnais-sance but apparently, they enjoyed the ride although gained no useful experience.[7]

The following day, 11 September, Henriques and Macpherson joined Archie Holford-Walker on a second reconnaissance this time guided by a Second Lieutenant from 6th Division. On this occasion they approached closer to the front line and gained some idea as to the shell deformed ground over which they would travel. However, they were around a thousand yards back from their battlescape and all they

3   Henriques, 'The Attack on the Quadrilateral'.
4   Ibid.,, p. 15.
5   Henriques, *Indiscretions of a Warden*, pp. 115-117.
6   H.Q. Fourth Army, Instructions for the Employment of 'Tanks', 11 September 1916 quoted in Pidgeon, *The Tanks at Flers*, p. 56.
7   Henriques, Lieut. B.L.Q: 'SECRET: Lecture on the Attack on the Quadrilateral', Bovington, 6 March1917.

The Bray Plateau and the site of the Loop Railway. (Author)

Ferme de Bronfay
Seigneurie de Braunfay

Ce site est riche d'un passé historique qui remonte à la guerre des gaulles, puisque c'est ici que se trouvait le passage entre la "France" et la "Belgique". Durant la Pax Romana, une villa Gallo Romaine serait déjà un vaste domaine. Des ruines sont visibles par vues aériennes derrière la ferme.

Plus près de nous, en 1916, les premiers chars partirent d'ici pour rejoindre le front à la Boisselle. Puis la ferme fut transformée en poste de secours et hôpital Anglais.

Entre deux guerres, Bronfay fut le centre d'un mouvement de protestation ouvrière, emmené par Mᵉ Salvaudon, qui réclamait l'établissement d'un font de pension individuel. Ce projet fut rejeté au profit du système de cotisation généralisée.

Occupation Allemande pendant la seconde guerre mondiale. Bronfay est aujourd'hui une exploitation agricole.

Bronfay Farm, the location where the first tanks were detrained. There is a mistake on the memorial plaque. The tanks that operated from Pozières detrained at Dernacourt not La Boiselle. (Author)

could see were the shells falling in the area. They tried to orientate themselves on the village of Guillemont but as Henriques wrote:

> I could see it nowhere. I asked the officer from the Division to point it out to me. He asked me if I could see a few stones 500 yards away as that was all that was left of the village of Guillemont. Such was the state of what would have been a valuable landmark.[8]

From Henriques' description they must have been standing close to the Maltz Horn Farm position. However, they learned that the 6th Division had secured a line from Leuze Wood north-westward to the almost undetectable summit known as the Ginchy Telegraph east-north-east of the village of that name. The Division antici-pated that by 15 September they would have pushed further forward to the sunken Ginchy – Morval road and have captured the formidable German defence system, the Quadrilateral, which the Germans called the *Sydow-Höhe*. Henriques summarised their poor preparation for reconnaissance when he wrote:

> We had no reconnaissance practice and no map reading... and we had no practice or lectures on the compass ... we had no signalling... we had no knowledge of the dissemination of available information that would be necessary for us as Tank Commanders, nor did we know what information we should be likely to require.[9]

They arrived back at the Loop at about 8:00 p.m. Later that evening at 10:30 p.m. they received their orders which they found had been changed. Unfortunately the 6th Division (The Sherwood Foresters of the 71st Brigade and the Suffolk Regiment, 16th Brigade) had failed to take the Quadrilateral and now occupied shell holes in no man's land. The tanks now had to capture this position on the way to attack Morval. Henriques and Macpherson spent half the night studying their amended orders. It was 3:00 a.m. on 13 September before they got to bed.

The Quadrilateral was located on the easterly extension of the high ground that ran from Thiepval to Pozières onto High Wood to the Ginchy Telegraph and was the extreme eastern flank of the Fourth Army's Flers – Courcelette operation. It was east of the village of Ginchy on the Morval road. It was linked to 'The Triangle' on the Ginchy-Lesboeufs road by 'Straight Trench' that ran north from the Quadrilateral and to Bouleaux ('Bully') Wood to the south-east by Beef Trench. Thus the position controlled an arc of 270 degrees from the wood to the Lesboeufs road. It was a defen-sive position that utilised the cutting of the single track railway line that crossed the gently rising ground.

8   Ibid.,
9   Ibid.,

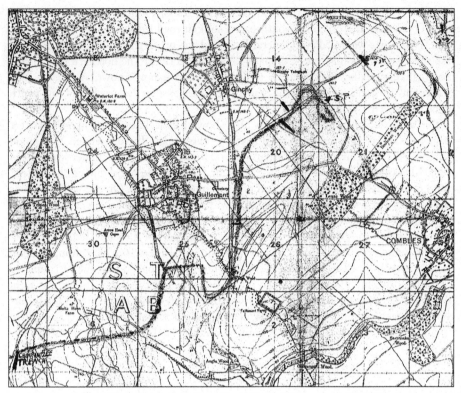

Map 4 Henriques' map of the Quadrilateral Operation. (TCMA)

Eventually by 5:00 p.m. on 13 September they had packed and were ready to start. However, much to Henriques' chagrin, he forgot the bird seed for the messenger pigeons! Their preparations were further hindered since neither Macpherson nor Henriques were supplied with their own maps, orders or timetables. They had to borrow their Section Commander's and memorise them. The only guidance as to the route to be taken was 'a set of aeroplane photographs' which 'might have been of inestimable value if only we had known how to look at it.'[10] Neither had seen such photographs before and certainly had not learned how to interpret them.

The initial destination of C Company (less No.1 Section tasked to attack Courcelette) was the Briqueterie close to the Montauban – Longueval crossroads and opposite Bernafay Wood. The journey was both tedious and hazardous although the distance from the Loop was in the region of only four miles. In all it took twelve and half hours to reach Chimpanzee Valley and its eponymous trench. Their average speed was

10 Ibid.,

a little over 3 mph. It was at the Briqueterie that Major Holford-Walker established his HQ. Nearby and off to the south-east a sunken road led down into Chimpanzee Valley. This was where Major General Ross and the 6th Division had their HQ and also the assembly point for C Company's 3 and 4 Sections. The northern part of this broad, shallow valley which led up to Trônes Wood is now known as the *Fond des Maras* and its continuation to the south the *Vallee de Bois Faviere*.[11] Aubrey Smith knew it as 'Death Valley.'[12]

The 'approach march' of the tanks also showed little knowledge of FSR Part 1 (pages 47-58) as they might have applied to the tanks. There it stated that 'good marching depends largely on the attention paid to march discipline, under which head is included everything that affects the efficiency of man and horse during the march.' (for 'horse' read 'tank').[13] They moved off in a long procession. On the way hundreds of Tommies witnessed their progress with wide eyes and humorous remarks. At this stage they were bombarded with questions not shells. Coincidently, Henriques met an officer from his and Macpherson's old regiment and passed through Henriques' elder brother Julian's regiment (The Queen's Westminster Rifles, 16th Battalion, London Regt.) destined for Leuze ('Lousy') Wood. During a stop he also met a couple of Oxford and Bermondsey Mission old boys who were in the Guards. It began to rain. Their tanks caused serious traffic jams along the length of the route during the night-time approach march: 'We found the need for night visual training as a great deal of our travelling was carried out at night ... night visual training was tremendously missed.'[14]

Humorous banter was soon replaced by strong language when they tore down telephone wires. The Assistant Provost Marshals and Military Police were not too pleased either. However, Henriques later drew some humour from the chaos he caused when he penned a cartoon to illustrate the situation.[15] Henriques confessed that 'the number of trees I broke and Motor Lorries I damaged and ammunition wagons I jammed was high. The traffic was jammed both ways for miles for 6 or 7 hours. We realised the need for careful road and route reconnaissance before movement is made by the tanks.'[16] They also learned that even over short distances tank tracks needed attention and petrol dumps were required along the route.

Henriques considered that the poor preparation for reconnaissance was inexcusable since 'nearly all of these things ... were on the syllabus.'[17] Two factors might explain this neglect. In the short space of time, six months, between establishing training at Elveden in England and at Yvrench and the Bray Plateau in France, any reconnaissance

11   Carte Topographique, Série Bleue, Bray-Sur-Somme, 2408E.
12   A Rifleman, *Four Years on the Western Front,* (London: Odhams Press, 1922), p. 174.
13   FRS Part 1, p. 47.
14   Ibid., p. 4.
15   Bovington Archives.
16   Henriques, The Attack on the Quadrilateral, p.9.
17   Ibid., p. 4.

A view down the sunken road into Chimpanzee Valley. The Malz Horn Plateau with Hardicourt aux Bois is visible on the right. (Author)

4 Section tanks in Chimpanzee Valley. The tall officer may well be Basil Henriques. (IWM Q5576)

Henriques' record of the approach march of the tanks. (TCMA)

training had to compete with priorities of basic driving, mechanics, crew training and firing practice.[18] 'The training of both officers and men was lamentably incomplete.'[19] In retrospect Henriques, as has been noted, regretted the time wasted on camouflaging the tanks and regarding their training as 'one huge game.' Training was not helped by the limited number of tanks available. Consequently 'we could not get... through many of the things that were on our programme.'[20] Henriques did not have his own tank until he reached France and then it broke down. Training for reconnaissance was also inhibited in both England and France by time spent demonstrating the new weapon to civil and military officialdom.

Even on the Bray Plateau

> Brigade had received orders that the tanks would perform daily from 9-10, & 2-3 (sic), and every officer within a large radius and an enormous number of the staff came to inspect us – we were an object of interest of everyone. This did not help with one's work.[21]

18   Williams-Ellises, *The Tank Corps*, pp. 19-20.
19   Browne, *The Tank in Action*, p.35.
20   Henriques, The Attack on the Quadrilateral, p. 3.
21   Ibid.,, p. 5.

His Company Commander, Major Allan Holford-Walker, concurred.[22] Henriques' later enthusiastic support for training was a response to these inadequacies.

The reconnaissance for Y/Z night (14/15 September) from their assembly point in Chimpanzee Valley to their 'jumping off' point was undertaken vicariously since it 'had been done by people we had never set eyes upon.'[23] His Company Commander was even more bitter about the poor route finding when he wrote:

> Gen. Gathorne-Hardy (XIV Corps Chief of Staff) … gave me a map showing the preconceived tank routes which had been arbitrarily fixed with no reconnaissance by any officer who knew anything about tanks at all.[24]

This was a reflection of the central problem of early tank operations. The new weapon was little understood by senior commanders who only regarded it as of auxiliary assistance to the infantry not as an independent arm with its own particularities to which they should adapt their plans.

Their advance was not helped by the infantry guide in front of Holford-Walker's tank who went ahead with a red and green light and 'kept on getting so far ahead of us that we continually lost contact.'[25] Henriques gave two divergent accounts of what took place in the next few hours and in a number of ways they are not consistent with one another. In his published memoir, *The Indiscretions of a Warden*, written nearly twenty years after the event, he had himself starting off behind Holford-Walker followed by Macpherson. An hour later Holford-Walker's tank was the first to break down with engine trouble in a 'kind of ravine' so he and George went on alone. They both reached their destination (unspecified but actually just short of the Guillemont cemetery crossroad, north of Wedge Wood) around midnight. This is where they left their tanks to undertake a personal reconnaissance on foot. They nearly crossed into no man's land before returning to their tanks and remained in each other's company where they 'chatted quietly until zero minus forty, when we set off.' Within ten minutes Macpherson's tank developed engine trouble and so Henriques had now to go on alone. This account owes more to fantasy than reality being fostered either by poor memory or in order to enhance Macpherson's reputation. In reality, confirmed by a report he penned two days after the events and his lecture in 1917, Macpherson's tank broke down twice within two hundred yards of the start in Chimpanzee Valley and was left behind.[26] The two remaining tanks crawled across the Malz Horn Plateau (Plaine des Neuf Moulins on modern maps) for about 1,500 yards keeping about 400 yards to the south of the remains of Malz Horn Farm and crossed the

---

22   NAM, Holford-Walker Papers, 32383.
23   Henriques, The Attack on the Quadrilateral, p. 10.
24   NAM, Holford-Walker Papers and quoted in Pidgeon, *The Tanks at Flers*, p. 57.
25   Ibid., p. 10.
26   Bovington Archives, Report dated 17.9.1916, Henriques file.

upper part of Wedge Wood (Angle Wood) Valley. The further they advanced the more difficult the path became and the slower the journey. They were continually backing up and manoeuvring to get out of the way of guns and other vehicles. At the Guillemont – Hardecourt road they turned north and crawled parallel to the road for about 1,100 yards until at about map reference T25 c 0,2 (see map 4) Holford-Walker and Henriques turned east into the head of the north-west fork of the 'Vallee de Quesne' (Wedge Wood [Angle Wood] Valley) about 550 yards south of the ruins of Guillemont. In following this route and in having to make a hair-pin turn south down into this narrow valley (the 'ravine' of the later account) Holford-Walker's tank broke the stub axle of its tail assembly (its 'hydraulic stabiliser'). There was no chance of a repair or replacement before zero hour. In the event, as noted earlier, it was discovered later that the tank could be driven without a hydraulic stabiliser. Henriques went on alone guided by his 'unhorsed' Section Commander. This was invaluable since he kept Henriques away from obstacles including shell holes in which there were live shells. They rounded the spur that separated the north-west fork from the north-east fork of the upper *Vallee de Quesne* (Wedge Wood [Angle Wood] Valley) and turned north to continue for about 1000 yards up its western slope. They passed 16th Brigade HQ in the quarry to the right and Wedge Wood about 100 yards further on. Henriques halted about 50 yards from the head of the valley in dead ground and before the cross roads by Guillemont cemetery at 11:45 p.m. (his jumping off point). The journey of two miles and three hundred yards had taken four and three quarter hours or about fifteen yards a minute. The tank had used up half of its petrol.

The distance to the German lines was still about 2000 yards. Holford-Walker volunteered to return to Chimpanzee Valley for additional fuel. Divisional Royal Engineer personnel assisted route finding for the tanks by taping the route from the jumping off point to the 'start line', where the track from Leuze Wood to Ginchy crossed the line of the railway. At midnight Henriques recalled doing 'my only bit of personal reconnaissance throughout the whole action' from the 'jumping off point' to the 'start point.' Even then he 'had difficulty in finding where the front British frontline was as the men in the shell holes did not seem to know.'[27] Already Henriques experience had taught him much which the infantry guides and Royal Engineers could not and which he would later employ as an RO in route preparation and guidance.[28]

In his solo attack in his female tank Henriques reached the Quadrilateral along one of the artillery free lane guided by the railway and its embankment at 6:05 a.m. Later it was discovered that although the Commander Royal Artillery (CRA) had been ordered to bombard the other lanes he failed to see the order and the consequences

---

27   Henriques, The Attack on the Quadrilateral, p. 11.
28   Ironically the first German tank (A7V) operations in 1918 also suffered from reconnaissance problems. See Ralf Raths, 'From the Bremerwagen to the A7V: German Tank Production and Armoured Warfare 1916-1918' in Searle (ed), *Genesis, Employment and Aftermath*, p. 101.

Wedge Wood Valley. (Author)

for the infantry were devastating. Henriques claimed that 'mine is the first tank in history to have fired on the enemy.'[29] He was probably mistaken since Captain Harold W. Mortimore of D Company in a male tank D1 ('Daredevil') attacked the enemy in the 'Brewery Salient' between Delville Wood and Ginchy at 5:30 a.m.[30] The railway embankment was the only landmark available together with the remains of telephone poles. He reached the Quadrilateral and managed to destroy a machine gun before the German machine guns and S.m.K (*Spitzgeschoss mit StahlKern*) armour piercing rounds penetrated the tank and destroyed both the periscope and prism rendering the vehicle virtually blind. Two of his crew were wounded and one sponson with its machine guns was put out of action whilst another machine gun suffered a blockage. Henriques was now bleeding from facial wounds and the tank was running out of petrol. He also feared its capture. The attack was an unmitigated disaster for the tanks and the 6th Division.[31] Poor reconnaissance as well as mechanical problems, the technical limitations of the tank including its restricted observation and vulnerability to armour-piercing bullets, late changes of plan as well as poor artillery targeting[32] and probably inadequate maps[33] combined with the inexperience of tank crews[34] all made their contribution to the failed attack.

29   L.L. Loewe, *Basil Henriques: A Portrait* (London, Routledge & Kegan Paul, 1976), p. 42.
30   Pidgeon, *The Tanks at Flers*, p. 148.
31   The present writer's second cousin, 19 year old Lance Corporal Cyril Heathcote, 1st Leicestershire Regiment, was killed in this attack..
32   Henriques, The Attack on the Quadrilateral, Appendix VI.
33   Pidgeon, *The Tanks at Flers*, pp. 84-85.
34   Henriques, The Attack on the Quadrilateral, p. 2.

Henriques returned to Wedge Wood where he met George in his repaired tank on the way to make a further attack on the Quadrilateral. In the event at 1:30 p.m. that attack was cancelled.[35] Henriques was immediately transferred via No. 14 Casualty Post to Casualty Clearing Station No. 48 at Grangetown, south-east of Méaulte. The medical staff, fearing that his eyes had been damaged, had him transferred to hospital in Rouen and back to England. Fortunately, after a short stay at the St. George's Eye Hospital, London, it appeared a false alarm and Henriques was discharged on 20 September. Hoping to return immediately to his unit he called upon Colonel Swinton at the War Office who had been informed of the events on 15 September whilst at Haig's forward HQ at Beauquesne. At the War Office Henriques learned that George Macpherson, after returning from the cancelled attack, had been killed outside 16 Brigade HQ probably by shell fire although it was alleged that he had committed suicide. This is the oft-repeated myth which has been challenged by the present writer (see above).

The consequence was that Henriques had a nervous breakdown which was probably exacerbated by 'post-traumatic stress disorder.' He was sent on leave to convalesce. In the New Year he returned to the recently established Tank Corps Depot at Wool (Bovington), Dorset and was then transferred to the new Reconnaissance Branch of the Corps. Here his experiences were used in training new officers.

In the meantime it would seem that C and D Companies quickly learned the lessons concerning reconnaissance. In the subsequent operations of the Somme campaign the remaining tanks adopted their own improvised reconnaissance arrangements:

> By this time the absolute necessity of good reconnaissance had been recognised: and before the action, tank commanders were taken to observation points from which they could see something of the ground beyond the front line. Landmarks were indicated to them, aeroplane photographs were studied, and, on zero night, the tank routes were taped as far as possible …[36]

On the 26 September, in preparation for the attack on Thiepval by two of the tanks of C Company, 'the entire crew of each tank reconnoitred the ground over which their advance was to be made and become acquainted with any landmarks available.'[37] Later, between 16 and 21 October, D Company Commander, Major F. Summers, led his tank commanders in a personal reconnaissance in the Achieux-Hébuterne-Auchonvillers area. He actually marked the routes on their maps.[38] A month later at Grandcourt a tank advance was cancelled because it was reported that: 'later reconnais-

---

35 Miles, *Military Operations, France and Belgium 1916, Volume 2*, p.314.
36 D. G. Browne, *The Tank in Action During the First World War*, (Leonaur, 2009 [1920]), p. 49.
37 T. Pidgeon, *Tanks on the Somme* (Barnsley, Pen & Sword Military, 2010), p. 88.
38 TNA, WO95/110, '4th Brigade Tank Corps, includes diary of D Coy Heavy Section, 01 August 1916-30 December 1919.'

sance of the ground, it has been found impracticable to use the routes **given** (emphasis added) for the tanks.'[39] However, it does suggest that the routes had once again been imposed on the tanks. A last improvised reconnaissance and guidance occurred on 19 November and was undertaken by the recently appointed GSO3 (Intelligence) as head of the nascent Reconnaissance Department of the HBMGC (see below).

Henriques concluded his lecture on 3 March 1917 with further impassioned support for the new tank organisation for training in personal reconnaissance, map reading, and understanding air photographs and to relating maps to the actual landscape.[40]

39 Pidgeon, *Tanks on the Somme*, p.102. It is not clear if reconnaissance was undertaken by tank personnel.
40 Henriques, The Attack on the Quadrilateral, p. 15.

6

Creation of a Legend

On 25 September 1916 the newly appointed Commanding Officer of the Tanks in France, Colonel H.J. Elles, wrote to the War Office confirming the initial establishment of the Tank HQ team. This consisted of a Deputy Assistant Adjutant (DAA) and Quarter Master General (QMG), (Capt. T. J. Uzelli), a Brigade Major (Capt. G. le Q. Martel) and Staff Captain (Capt. Capper). The HQ was initially established at Beauquesne, north of Amiens. This location was also Haig's advanced HQ during the Somme campaign. On 16 October Tank Corps HQ was transferred to Bermicourt, between St. Pol and Hesdin, north of the N39. This location together with the neighbouring villages became the scene of Tank Corps activity for the rest of the war.

Some members of Elles's staff in 1917; L to R Major Fuller, Capt. Uzielli, Lieut. Col. Elles, Capt. Atkin-Berry, Capt. Dundas, Capt. Butler. (TCMA)

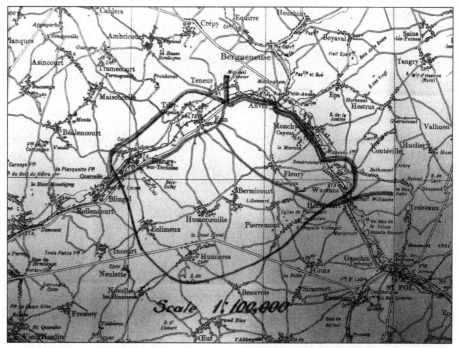

Map 5 The original map showing the location of the Tank HQ at Bermicourt and the villages used by the Tank Corps. (TNA)

Capt. G.le Q. (later Lieut. General)
Martel. (Author's collection)

Later in December they were joined by Major J.F.C. Fuller as General Staff Officer 1 (GSO1). Elles continued:

> The G.S.O.3 (I) will be appointed in a day or two as soon as we can get the right man. This officer will not be for secret service, espionage, prisoners, censorship or that sort of I work, but for ground work, such as roads, approaches, obstacles, aeroplane photographs, and maps.[1]

The intention, therefore, was to place as much emphasis on reconnaissance of the British side of the hill as the enemy's side.

Capt. Fredrick Elliot ('Boots') Hotblack was the 'right man' and he was 'handpicked' by Elles for the job. Hotblack overheard Brigadier J. Charteris, Haigh's Intelligence Chief, tell Elles that 'the Chief (Haig) has issued instructions that you can pick your staff ... You can pick anyone you like. I got the job.'[2]

A Legend: this is how Clough Williams-Ellis described him in both a letter dated 5 January 1918 congratulating Hotblack on gaining a bar to his MC and in his autobiography. He wrote that

> ... my immediate superior in Tank Corps reconnaissance and intelligence was Major (later General) 'Boots' Hotblack ... His legendary gallantry, experience, tireless enterprise and energy made him the very pattern of the good soldier. Always good humoured and helpful however exhausted, we others could not but strive, however vainly, to live up to his example. One thing he did for me was to make the war more interesting through his own intense absorption and keenness. The other, though it did not make me 'brave' in his own rare way, taught me to be at least fatalistically unafraid in tight places.[3]

The reference to his bravery was no exaggeration since he was decorated six times including the Distinguished Service Order (DSO) and Bar and the Military Cross (MC) and Bar, Legion of Honour (5th Class) and the Russian Order of St. Anne inscribed 'For Valour in War'.[4] He was Mentioned in Dispatches (MID) four times (17 February and 22 June 1915, 15 May 1917 and 25 May 1918). Even then some felt he was under decorated.[5] He was wounded five times. Hotblack, though born in Norwich was living in Lewes, Sussex, when he volunteered for the army in

1   TNA, WO158/836, War Office, Military Headquarters; Correspondence and Papers, First World War, FRANCE, BELGIUM AND GERMANY, GENERAL HEADQUARTERS, tanks, 01 September1916-31 October 1916. 'I' is Intelligence.
2   TCMA, Hotblack Papers, Box 1, 19876(2), Letter to Martin Gilbert, 28 Nov. 1968.
3   Williams-Ellis, *Architect Errant*, p.127.
4   According to the *Northampton Mercury* on 9 February 1923 this was a 'fine record ... not achieved by any other Captain in the British Army.'
5   Undated letter of appreciation written by Brigadier George M.O. Davy, CB, CBE, DSO.

Major. F.E. ('Boots') Hotblack.
(TCMA)

August 1914 (no. P/15316) when he was 27. He was granted a temporary General List commission in Intelligence on 2 September as a Temporary Second Lieutenant (Special Appointment). He landed in France on 12 September 1914. Later he was to be followed by his two younger brothers, Gerald (Welch Regiment) and Harold (Royal Field Artillery).[6] His rapid involvement in the war may owe something to the work of Colonel George M. W. Macdonogh, the head of the Special Duties Section of the Director of Military Operations (DMO) at the War Office, who had followed the advice of Brigadier David Henderson. In 1912 Macdonogh

> … started to compile a list of linguists and others possessing skills likely to be of value in intelligence work on the Continent. These men, all of whom were civilians, would be asked to join the Intelligence Corps if and when Britain went to war … On 5 August 1914, within hours of Britain's declaration of war against Germany, the War Office sent out telegrams to report to Southampton, and practically overnight, the Intelligence Corps sprang to life.[7]

6   The fourth and youngest brother, Geoffrey, died of wounds received 'in action against Irish Rebels at Cross Berry, Co. Cork' in 1920 (*Sussex Agricultural Express*, 1 January 1921).

7   Thomas G. Fergusson, *British Military Intelligence 1870-1914* (MD: University Publications of America, Inc., 1984), pp. 178-181. Quoted in Jeffrey D. Schnakenburg (Major USAF), 'The Limits of Intelligence: the Role of Intelligence in Great Britain's Response to Technological and Doctrinal Surprise during World War I' (sic), (unpublished M.Sc. thesis submitted to the faculty of the National Intelligence University, 2013), pp.

Hotblack was fluent in both German and French resulting from an education at Geneva University in Switzerland and spending two years in the Rhineland, Germany. Previously he was at school at St. Mark's, Windsor (later incorporated in the Imperial Service College and later still Haileybury) where he passed the Oxford Local examination in 1903 aged sixteen[8] and at Brighton College where he trained as an accountant.[9] Consequently he was 'head hunted' for the 'Intelligence Corps' where initially he, with other Intelligence Officers, all of whom lacked military training 'were employed chiefly as dispatch riders to help keep contact with the French Forces'.[10] In particular he was appointed to Field Marshal Sir John French's General Head Quarters (GHQ) as liaison officer to Castelnau's II French Army. He was to serve in all the major BEF operations from the Marne in 1914 to the breach of the Hindenburg Line during the 'Hundred Days', 28 September 1918. It was at this time in 1914 that he apparently received a wound from the bayonet point of an elderly French Territorial sentry whilst motor cycling at night through the Villers Cotterêt Forest during the Battle of the Marne. He is alleged to have plugged the wound with cotton wool taken from his distraught assailant.[11] On 28 October 1914 he was attached to Sir Douglas Haig's I Corps during the First Battle of Ypres. He came under the command of Major John Charteris, Haig's General Staff Officer for Intelligence. Following the First Ypres and the withdrawal of I Corps from the line Hotblack was transferred on 4 December to IV Corps commanded by Lieutenant General Sir Henry Rawlinson then based at Merville. Later in 1915 he was 'head hunted' by Charteris and Haig and returned to their command which was now First Army HQ. Under Rawlinson he served at Neuve Chapelle and Festubert (where he was attached to 'Barter Force' and was 'only slightly wounded in the left hand and has now resumed his duties'[12]) and under Haig at Loos and the Somme.[13]

57-58. See also Jim Beach, *Haig's Intelligence, GHQ and the German Army, 1916-1918*, (Cambridge, University Press, 2013), p. 68.

8   *Reading Mercury*, 17 June 1916 that the Imperial Service College proudly recorded the award of the MC to its former St. Mark's pupil and earlier his examination success on 22 August 1903.

9   He was employed in the family brewing business.

10   The Intelligence Corps Museum & Archives (ICMA), Chicksands, Bedfordshire, Hotblack Papers, Accession No. 199, p. 1.

11   Ken Chadwick, "Boots": The Call for Service (*The Tank*, Vol. 57, 1974, pp.513-517). This reference is not sourced by Ken Chadwick and there is no reference to this wound in his military papers kept at the Army Personnel Centre, Glasgow or by General Elles. There is greater evidence for the subsequent wounds that are indicated by his five wound stripes (see photograph).

12   *Sussex Express, Surrey Standard* and *Kent Mail*, Friday, 11 June 1915. The short report included a photograph of Hotblack in uniform. His cap badge was that of an officer commissioned in the General List.

13   'Barter's Force was an ad hoc grouping of 1st and 47th Division formed on 13 May. They got their name from the CO-Maj Gen Barter (GOC 47th Div.'(sic) (Dr Spencer Jones). This wound was the first to be officially recorded.

Hotblack modestly claimed not to know why Haig wanted him especially as he felt useless as an untrained Intelligence Officer during the First Ypres battle. He could only put it down to 'a light hearted remark, made during the dark days of the Battle, which made Sir Douglas Haig laugh and laughs were in short supply at that time.'[14] His appointment raised issues about the responsibility for Intelligence personnel. The controversy was whether Intelligence Corps officers should be posted to specific units or retained by Higher Command and directed by them 'to lower formations and moved about according to the military situation (or the wishes of John Charteris)'.[15] The issue went as far as the War Office without any apparent solution except that Haig 'pulled rank' and Hotblack was posted to First Army on 21 August 1915 and eventually accompanied Haig and Charteris to GHQ of the British Expeditionary Force (BEF) in 1916 after Haig became its Commander in Chief. Underpinning the problem was the shortage of good Intelligence Officers which made the talented Hotblack such an asset. He was concerned that he had courted controversy which might affect his military career but was reassured by Brigadier General Whigham, the Deputy Chief of the Imperial General Staff (DGIGS) of the War Office. Whilst Hotblack was giving him a conducted tour of the Somme battlefield:

Whigham said that he had wanted to have a look at me because he was all-too-familiar with my name as there had been a fat file going round the War Office, dealing with my services. I made some apologetic remark, and he said: "You have no cause to worry, with John Charteris and a couple of the Bold Bad Barons (Corps Commanders) competing for your services, you have had a first class advertisement."[16]

Hotblack's role was 'Battle Liaison for Intelligence', however, he was employed by Charteris 'on a considerable number of jobs, not always strictly Intelligence', for instance, talking to War Correspondents or the French. Although he had a car and driver he used a motor cycle to get about since it was quicker on the congested roads unless of course, he fell off which he did on at least one occasion. Consequently, when King George V visited GHQ Hotblack sported a black eye when he was presented to him.

He decided to become a regular officer so on 9 June 1915 'he obtained a regular commission in the Norfolk Regiment, and in October 1918 became a captain in the Northamptonshire Regiment, although serving in the wartime Tank Corps' as a Temporary Major.[17]

14 ICMA, Hotblack, p.2
15 ICMA, Hotblack, p.2.
16 ICMA, Hotblack. p.2.
17 LHMA, Hotblack Papers, Sir Basil Liddell Hart, 'Draft Times obituary of Major General F. E. Hotblack', February 1968.

Between 3 March and 3 June 1916 he went 'under cover' as an 'ordinary Intelligence Officer' to the British Mission to the Belgian Army at La Panne on the coast. The Mission was led by Prince Alexander of Teck. It was probably for this work that he was awarded his first MC that was gazetted on 8 June 1916 although a citation appears never to have been published perhaps because of the clandestine nature of his work. He never spoke about the reason he was awarded this decoration even to his family. There is, however, an unsubstantiated suggestion in the family that he 'worked behind the lines'. If this was the case the supposition is that Hotblack's purpose might have been to inform GHQ about this location and the Allied lines with a view to a British landing on the Belgian coast (Operation 'Hush'). This was to take place in conjunction with any British offensive that might take place in the Ypres salient. This idea was taken forward in the preparations for the Third Ypres campaign in 1917 but later dismissed. Hotblack had reported on the unfavourable conditions for any sea-borne invasion which included the possible enfilading of Ostend harbour by German artillery. His reconnaissance and study of large scale maps showed the complicated system of land drainage north-east of Ypres which would and did prove vulnerable to a prolonged artillery barrage. This was valuable experience for his subsequent role in the Tank Corps.

It will be useful here to recount for comparison Hotblack's description of his role whilst an Intelligence Corps Officer in the light of his future appointment as a Tank Corps Intelligence Officer. He summarised it as follows:

a. General. To provide intelligence on the enemy, his tactics, morale and weapons, and of enemy occupied territory, to the commander and staff of formation to which they are attached. To form a link in the flow of intelligence from the forward areas back to GHQ and vice versa.

b. The first examination of prisoners and captured documents to find out if our attack had been expected. (Battles of Neuve, Chapells (sic), Fromelles, Festubert and Loos.) Raids were also carried out by our infantry in order to capture prisoners for identification of units opposite our front and for the establishment of the German Order of Battle. Success in these tasks depended in a great measure upon how much the examining officer already knew about the enemy.

c. Investigation of reports that enemy snipers were active behind our lines. These always turned out to be long range fire from the enemy lines, which in the course of fighting, had many salients. Moreover the Germans had nearly always remained in possession of the high ground.

d. Investigation of the possibility of the enemy using the tunnels of coal mines, which in places ran under the front lines. These had, however, been effectively blocked.

e. Examination of early aeroplane photographs. It was usually possible, at first glance, to tell which were our lines and which were those of the enemy because the latter showed up strongly with clear communication trenches, whereas our lines looked comparatively weak and sketchy. (Digging was not a popular pastime with the British soldier.)[18]

It is clear that both Haig and Elles, who had been delegated by his C in C to report on the first tank trials at Elveden and Hatfield, had a high regard for Hotblack. This feeling was reciprocated. One encounter between Hotblack and Haig showed a side of the 'Chief' that is rarely considered. Hotblack claimed that although 'I was very junior and seldom reported to him personally, but I saw enough of him to know that he was not indifferent and callous about the very heavy casualties that were incurred when he commanded I Corps and later when he was commander in chief (sic)'[19] He had a personal experience which reinforced his regard for Haig. During the opening of the Arras offensive on 9 April 1917 Hotblack was wounded (his second) in the head by a shell and his Reconnaissance Officer companion, Captain T.A. Nelson, scion of the well-known Edinburgh publishing house, was killed. He was evacuated to No. 1 Red Cross Hospital at Le Touquet established by the Duchess of Westminster. Although his head wounds appeared superficial, there was a concern that his skull was fractured. It was rumoured that he was to be evacuated to England and therefore, following the usual practice, would cease to be on the strength of the BEF. He feared that it might be a year before he could return to the Front. In the meantime he would be used as an instructor with the newly formed Tank Units at Bovington Camp. Clearly this was not to his liking so he took his uniform, which contrary to regulations he had hidden under his bed, went 'into the bathroom, dressed and escaped through a window'.[20] He walked in the snow the five miles to GHQ at Montreuil and ordered a car to return him to Tank HQ at Bermicourt. He was clearly suffering from concussion. However, he was intercepted by Brigadier Charteris who had been instructed by Haig to make enquires about Hotblack at the hospital. They had reported that he had serious head injuries and was being evacuated to England. Charteris, therefore, placed him under open arrest to await a return to the hospital under escort.

At the hospital he was informed that he would be court-marshalled for being Absent Without Leave (AWOL). His position 'was probably made worse by some wag of a medical officer at GHQ who had telephoned the Hospital to say that they had heard that the Hospital was trying out a new treatment for head injuries which apparently involved the patient wandering about in snow storms'.[21] Haig saved the situation by pointing out to the Commandant of the Hospital that he would not confirm any court-marshal decision especially of a person whose aim was to head for the frontline not away from it. Instead he granted Hotblack leave, allowing him to convalesce in the

---

18 ICMA, Hotblack, p.1. It is instructive to read this alongside Dr James Beach's *Haig's Intelligence*.
19 Intelligence Corps Museum & Archives, Hotblack Papers, (accession no. 514), p. 1.
20 ICMA, Hotblack Papers, p. 1.
21 Ibid., p. 2.

UK, and so remain on the strength of the BEF and Tank Corps. He returned to duty 1 May but was again 'wounded on duty' on 7 July 1917, (wound number three), on this occasion it was a leg wound.[22] However, in the best British stiff upper lip tradition, it was reported that 'he hopes that his injury is so slight that he will not be idle for long ... he trusts he will not have to go to hospital and waste his time.'[23]

Many years later on 5 June 1970 he was interviewed by a BBC researcher preparing a television Horizon programme on the tanks' contribution to the Battle of Cambrai (November 1917). During the interview he admitted that

> though I thought I could judge things objectively now, I might be a little preju-diced about Haig ...he helped me with kindness and understanding. The B.B.C. Representative gasped and changed the subject. He had, I expect, seen Joan Littlewood's film "Oh what a lovely War (sic)". I did suggest that he might consult Miss Littlewood as an expert on Warfare, but my irony was lost on him.[24]

Six months before the Battle of Arras Hotblack had responded with alacrity to Elles' 'job specification' (see above). At Tank Corps HQ he gained Fuller's sobriquet of 'a lover of beauty and battles, a mixture of Abelard and Marshal Ney'. Whilst it is not difficult to understand the allusion to Ney and a 'Lover of Battles', his decorations and wound stripes are testament to that, and Abelard, the peripatetic medieval scholar who wandered across northern France, the reference being a 'Lover of Beauty' is more obscure since apparently there was no Eloise in sight. It may have been a reference to his aesthetic appreciation of both the landscape and the Arts.[25] Indeed Hotblack remained a life-long bachelor. His nickname of 'Boots' was a consequence perhaps of his penchant for wearing soft soled boots as recommended by Baden-Powell although there is a further suggestion that it was a reference to his permanently highly polished footwear.[26]

One of his first acts as GSO3(I) demonstrated his courage in battle. On 13 November, in the last tank operations of 1916 on the Somme a single tank, commanded by Lieutenant Partington, made an attack on the 'triangle', a German position between

22   A list of Hotblack's military activities that accompanied a letter from Brigadier General Elles to GHQ dated 15 April 1918 included in Hotblack's military papers at Army Personnel Centre, Historical Disclosures, Glasgow.
23   *Sussex Agricultural Express*, 20 July 1917.
24   Intelligence Corp Museum, Hotback Papers. This has no accession number but is entitled: RECOLLECTIONS-F.E.HOTBLACK. CONFIDENTIAL. B.B.C. T.V. PROGRAMME ON TANKS. The film, of course, was actually produced by Sir Richard Attenborough and was based on the Joan Littlewood's controversial stage production.
25   This opinion was expressed by his great nephew, Geoffrey Hotblack, in conversation with the author.
26   Baden-Powell, *Scouting for Soldiers and NCOs*, p. 43. Apparently in East Anglia there was also a shoemaker who before the war made and advertised 'Hotblacks Gentlemen's Health Boots' in *The Bury Free Press*, 7 November 1885.

The *Graphic* picture paper's melodramatic reconstruction of Hotblack guiding a single tank in November 1916 with his highly polished boots. (TCMA)

The Teacher of the Tank

TEMPORARY CAPTAIN FREDERICK ELLIOTT HOTBLACK, INTELLIGENCE CORPS AND ATTACHED TO THE MOTOR GUN C
DED A TANK INTO ACTION BY WALKING IN FRONT OF IT UNDER VERY HEAVY FIRE. HE DISPLAYED GREAT COU
AND DETERMINATION THROUGHOUT, AND NOW ADDS A D.S.O. TO HIS M.C.

the villages of Beaumont Hamel and Beaucourt on the right bank of the Ancre. Hotblack had undertaken a reconnaissance and taped the route the previous evening. However, an overnight snow shower had obscured the tape. Hotblack proceeded 'to guide the tank … by actually leading the tank forward by walking in front of it, despite the hail of enemy bullets aimed at the tank – and therefore at him.'[27] In fact Hotblack took advantage of the protection afforded by shell holes although they were full of ice and water. Afterwards, Partington's tank was needed to support another infantry attack. Since there was no other way of communicating with Partington

> … again Major (sic) Hotblack came forward and again he crossed the fire-swept zone undeterred. He reached the Tank and piloted it back behind our lines,

27   Trevor Pidgeon, *Tanks on the Somme: From Morval to Beaumont Hamel*, p. 148.

An Unmilitary Hotblack.
(*Daily Mirror*, 11 January
1917)

GUIDED A TANK — FINE DEEDS BY OFFICERS.

Captain Frederick Elliott Hotblack, M.C., who has now been awarded the D.S.O. He guided a tank into action by walking in front of it under very heavy fire. The gallant officer, who is attached to a machine-gun section, displayed great courage and determination.

where a renewed attack was planned … It was for this remarkable piece of work that Major Hotblack was awarded his D.S.O. (sic).[28]

His action was applauded in the *News of the World* and *Daily Mirror* on 11 January 1917 and was accompanied by his photograph whilst the *Graphic* later published the full page melodramatic reconstruction of the action. Hotblack complained successfully to the *News of the World* and *Daily Mirror*, through his solicitor, that the photographs were published without his permission. Both newspapers published an apology.[29] In response to the *Graphic* illustration his solicitor wrote that 'this, no doubt, is purely an imaginary picture and I do not see how any objection can be taken to it.' The question arises as to why Hotblack should object to the publication of his photograph. Setting aside the possibility of undue modesty, it is possible that as an Intelligence Officer who

28   Williams-Ellises, *The Tank Corps*, p. 37. At the time of these actions Hotblack was still a captain.
29   Letter from Edward W. Candler, solicitor, to Hotblack, 30 January 1917. Source: Geoffrey Hotblack.

would be required to work close to the frontline anonymity was critical. However, this suggestion is not borne out by the earlier publication of his photograph in uniform in 1915 and the reference to his role in Intelligence. The 1917 photographs are of a much younger clean shaven man in civilian clothes who is unrecognisable as the martial figure that appeared in the press on 11 June 1915 nineteen months earlier. Hotblack may have been more concerned that he did not project a military image.

Clough Williams-Ellis believed these inspiring actions were critical in establishing a standard of competence and conduct and 'much of the subsequent efficiency of the Reconnaissance Branch of the Tank Corps may be traced to this incident. Reconnaissance took its proper place, it was recognised as a fighting service and its work was seen to be a necessary preliminary to every action.'[30] Hotblack acknowledged that in these early experiences he had learned a great deal, some of which he was able to pass on to Fuller for purposes of training future ROs.

Awarded a bar to his DSO a year later during the Battle of Cambrai (gazetted 12 February 1918), Hotblack had been tasked by Brigadier Elles to observe the actions of the 1st Tank Brigade on the left wing of the attack.[31] The citation reads:

> For conspicuous gallantry on November 23 during the attack on Fontaine-Notre Dame. By his personal example and initiative he carried on the attack, reorganising the infantry, whose officers had become casualties, and collecting tanks. He had to pass through a heavy barrage and was continuously under machine-gun fire, but succeed in launching a fresh attack with tanks and infantry. This officer has been present throughout the four great battles of the year, except Arras, where he was wounded on the first day. He has shown throughout persistent gallantry and contempt of danger in the pursuance of his duty as a reconnaissance and battle liaison officer which has been an inspiration to all ranks.[32]

The citation for the bar to his MC is equally detailed. The action occurred as British and American forces attacked the Hindenburg (Siegfried) Line over the St. Quentin Canal tunnel in the area between Vendhuile and Bellicourt in September 1918:

> Lieut. (T. Major) HOTBLACK, FREDERICK ELLIOT DSO MC Headquarters Tank Corps. Awarded Bar to MC. For conspicuous gallantry, initiative and devotion to duty near Quennemont Farm on the morning of September 29 1918. This officer who is GSO2 Intelligence, was following up the operations when the mist lifted and disclosed a strongly held enemy position dominating the advance to the south. He at once ran across two tanks and directed them on

---

30   Williams-Ellises, Ibid., p. 37-38.
31   Majors Martel and Boyd-Rochford observed 2nd and 3rd Tank Brigades respectively.
32   R.F.G. Maurice (ed.), *Tank Corps Book of Honour* (Uckfield,, The Naval & Military Press Ltd. reprint of 1919 edition), p. 115.

this strong point, himself going into action in one of the Tanks to make certain of success. The position was later found to be the actual German front line and was strongly held by machine guns with field guns in close support. The Tanks met with strong opposition and the heavy machine-gun fire made it impossible for the gunners in the Tanks to work their guns, though the enemy were at close quarters and exposing themselves freely. Major Hotblack then opened the revolver loopholes and fired his revolver into the enemy repeatedly; driving them off. He was wounded in the eyes and temporarily blinded. The two Tanks of which he was in charge were knocked out by shellfire and his crews were almost all wounded. When the position had been cleared of the enemy Major Hotblack in spite of his wounds at once got the wounded into safety and organised a hurried defence with a few infantry against a possible counter attack. The very prompt and gallant action of this officer overcame a situation which would in all probability have held up our advance to the south of QUENNEMONT farm.[33]

Had a more senior officer witnessed this action then he may have received a higher decoration. This was his fifth wound and followed a fourth received between the opening of the Battle of Amiens and 25 August 1918.[34] The attack on the Bellicourt Tunnel was his last action in the Great War as his wounds were such that he was transferred to England blinded permanently in the right eye.[35] Another RO, Captain Norman Musgrave (Mark) Dillon, confirmed that Hotblack 'was the most outstanding of the staff at Berlesmont (sic). He was a man of the most astonishing bravery' but there is a tinge of criticism when he continued 'he had no need to go near the battle ... because he was a staff officer.' There is also an implicit criticism that the act of leading a tank into action set a precedent so that during the Battle of Arras Dillon had 'to take over a tank whose officer had been killed leading his tank over perfectly good ground ... and it became a craze'.[36]

By 20 October 1916 the War Office acceded to Elles' request to expand Tank Corps establishment which would then allow the posts of Battalion and Company ROs to be created.[37] The next task was to appoint the reconnaissance officers.

33   Maurice, *Tank Corps Book of Honour,* p. 208.
34   Letter dated 25 August 1918 from Major-General H. Elles to GHQ. (Army Personnel Centre, Glasgow). The Centre is not allowed to release the medical history of individuals hence it was necessary to piece together details of his wounds from various other sources.
35   A photograph of Hotblack taken around 1960 shows him with a piratical black patch over his right eye thus lending support to Beach's description of 'Scouting for Brigands'.
36   Brotherton Library (Special Collections), University of Leeds also the Imperial war Museum (9752).
37   TNA, WO158/849, Letter from the War Office to GHQ. 20 October 1916.

7

Gifted Amateurs

When the Tank Corps went into action on 15 September 1916 it operated with two companies, B and C. By February 1917 it had expanded to two Brigades each of four Battalions. In April a third Brigade was created. Each Brigade normally had three Battalions which were given the letters A to I in succession. After Cambrai they were re-designated 1 to 9. Each Battalion had three Companies. The Battalions at Cambrai (20 November 1917) were not distributed evenly across the Brigades. Whilst 1st Brigade had three Battalions (D, E and G), 2nd Brigade consisted of only two (B and H). 3rd Brigade then had four Battalions (A, C, F and I). The Companies were named consecutively through the corps (1 to 27) not by Battalion. Companies were composed usually of four Sections. When the Tank Corps appointed Intelligence/Reconnaissance officers their ranks corresponded to this organisational structure: the HQ GSO 2 (Intelligence) and Brigade Intelligence Officers were majors; Battalion Reconnaissance Officers were captains and Company Reconnaissance Officers were subalterns. As mentioned earlier the ranks reflected pay grades not roles.[1] They were at least one rank below their unit commander. As also noted above the War Office had already acceded to Elles' request to expand the Tank Corps establishment which had then allowed the posts of Battalion and Company ROs to be created.[2] The training of these new ROs was a priority (see below). Although 'Bermicourt was embryonic in November 1916... schools were urgently needed and were fairly quickly improvised. Uzielli did wonders'.[3] The other task was to appoint the ROs.

Initially the ROs, like other Tank Corps personnel, were drawn unsystematically from volunteers from other units already engaged in France.[4] Beach suggests that because of 'the very fragmentary survival of personnel records, it is impossible

---

1   WO158/836, Military Headquarters, Correspondence and Papers 1 September 1916-31 October 1916, letter dated 20 October 1916.
2   TNA, WO158/849, Letter from the War Office to GHQ, 20 October 1916.
3   LHCMA, 9/28/43, Letter from Hotblack to Liddell Hart, 22 March 1948.
4   NAM, Holford-Walker Papers.

to discern any clear pattern in their selection for these roles.'[5] The physical criteria, together with the requirement that volunteers should have 'a high standard of intelligence', were established by the War Office.[6] Volunteering was idiosyncratic. Every volunteer had his own motive for transferring to the Tanks but few had the aptitude to become ROs.[7] The manner in which Capt. Williams-Ellis, an Intelligence Officer in the Welsh Guards, volunteered for the Tank Corps has been recounted when he 'boldly called upon the Commanding Officer, a joy riding subaltern in a dubiously borrowed car, with no better credentials than a (my) highly unofficial and impertinent curiosity', had tea with Elles, and later 'put in for a Tank Section.' Henriques,

Capt. D.G. Browne 1933-34.
(Andrew Burton)

originally a Tank Commander, became an RO by default after being wounded on 15 September 1916. He claimed that at Bovington his 'C. O. quickly realized that I should not be much good at teaching tank mechanics to recruits. I was, therefore, made reconnaissance officer'.[8] His size must have also been a handicap. He did, however, as has been illustrated, possess a talent for drawing. Similarly Captain Douglas Gordon Browne began his career in the Tank Corps as a Tank Commander before transferring to the Tank Reconnaissance Branch.

Browne attested for the Royal Fusiliers in London on 29 August 1914 and joined them at Colchester. His 'Trade or Calling' was 'Author.[9] His original number was 348. He was thirty years of age and born in Willesden, Middlesex and educated at Westminster School. He was half an inch under six foot and weighed in at twelve stone. On 11 January 1915 he was made lance corporal (unpaid). He saw Home Service principally in the 107th Training Battalion at Marine Gardens, Portobello, Edinburgh and then with 10th Service Battalion, Royal Fusiliers before he was posted to the 31st Battalion on 9 June 1915. At the time it was the Reserve Company, 18th Battalion,

5   Beach, 'Scouting for Brigands' in Searle, *Genesis, Employment, Aftermath*, p. 115.
6   TNA, WO158/849.
7   Browne, Dillon and Henriques as ROs complained that many tank commanders and some unit commanders could not read maps.
8   Henriques, *The Indiscretions of a Warden*, p. 124.
9   Methuen published his book entitled *Christ and his Age* (1913).

Royal Fusiliers stationed at Windmill Hill, Andover.[10] He applied for a commission in the Royal Welsh Fusiliers on 29 June 1916 and became an Officer Cadet on 2 August 1916 first at the 9th Scottish Cadet Battalion at Gailes Camp then at the Cadet Unit of the Machine Gun Corps at Bisley on 1 October 1916. There is no explanation why Browne should choose the Royal Welsh Fusiliers. It is, therefore, mere idle speculation to note that as an author he may have felt an affinity with the Regiment that included the literary figures Siegfried Sassoon, Robert Graves, Wyn Griffiths and David Jones amongst its numbers. He was commissioned on 23 November 1916 and at the same time formally transferred to the Machine Gun Corps (under probation). This was still the Heavy Branch of the Machine Gun Corps (HBMGC) the forerunner of the Tank Corps. He then moved to the recently established tank depot and training ground at Bovington with other recently commissioned officers, often from the ranks, for his basic training as a tank commander.

He arrived in France on 25 May 1917 following his appointment to 21 Company, G Battalion, 1st Tank Brigade at Bermicourt. Together with F Battalion they were the first two new tank units raised in England to go to France. Without his own tank, now Mark IVs, he first commanded the fifth or reserve crew. After two years and nearly eight months Browne had not seen action but only heard the guns at Messines.

He had not long to wait as within the month the 1st Tank Brigade had moved to Oosthoek Wood north of Poperinghe to prepare for the Third Ypres campaign. As a tank commander he was in one of the two Companies of his Brigade to see action on the 31 July 1917 in support of XVIII Corps (Lieutenant General Sir Ivor Maxse). In the role of tank commander he undertook the reconnaissance of the route determined by the Battalion RO from Oosthoek Wood that is described in Chapter 10. It is instructive to compare this reconnaissance with that of Henriques a year earlier. Both were tank commanders who eventually became Company ROs. One was poorly trained in the skills of reconnaissance and was led by ill-informed infantrymen prior to the introduction of the specialist trained RO. The other had the advantage of following where the experts led even though the route was subject to shelling.[11] On 31 July Browne advanced in his new tank, G46 'Gina' (appropriately a 'female' tank), across the Pilkem Ridge before 'bellying' close to the northern edge of Kitchener Wood. This resulted in a long trek back on foot to Oosthoek Wood. On 19 August he participated in the successful 'Cockroft' operation (see Chapter 3) in a replacement tank G47 'Gitana'.

Although he had been given a third tank, 'Goliath', for a proposed attack on Spriet, on the Poelcapelle-Westroosebeke road, this was to be Browne's final operation in the salient as a tank commander. However, the attack was cancelled. He left the salient in late October for Wailly, mainly used as a tank driving school, near Arras but not before being hospitalised on 6 October for two weeks with diarrhoea. He had a

10   TNA, WO339/60279.
11   Browne, *The Tank in Action*, pp. 121-128.

second bout of ill-health which kept him out of the iconic tank offensive at Cambrai commencing 20 November 1917. He was confined to hospital between 5 November and 20 December with influenza followed by myalgia or generalised muscle pain which was often a consequence of a virus.

In January 1918, whilst the 1st Tank Brigade settled at the tankodrome on the Bray Plateau, Browne transferred from Tank Commander to Reconnaissance Officer. This was as a part of a series of promotions consequent on his Battalion Commander, Lieutenant Colonel E.B. Hankey, being promoted to command the new 4th Tank Brigade. Browne succeeded Henriques as RO of 1 (A) Company, 7th Battalion, since apparently he claims that the work had always appealed to him. On 2 February 1918 he was granted his first leave which was extended to 23 February.[12] He returned to find that the 1st Tank Brigade, now a part of the First Army, had moved to Artois. His Battalion (7th) was established to the west of Bully in the mining area of Bouvigny-Boyeffles. His reconnaissance work, which included Vimy Ridge, was initially protective in preparation for the German Spring Offence. They prepared to undertake counter attacks in this area. However, these attacks never took place since this area was by-passed in the German Spring Offensive although they still suffered frequent shelling.[13]

On 24 May 1918 he was promoted to full lieutenant. One consequence of Browne's Tank Brigade being located in Artois was that it did not participate in either of the Hamel, Moreuil or Amiens offensives. Browne was also on leave between 18 July and 2 August. It was during the 'Hundred Days' that he saw more action as a Company RO, first with the Third Army north of Bapaume between 21 August and 4 September. This was followed by support for the Canadians and the First Army around Bourlon and Sancourt, west of Cambrai, between 25 and 30 September. It was for assisting the Canadians in crossing the Canal du Nord that he was awarded a Military Cross:

> For conspicuous gallantry and devotion to duty. He showed great skill and ability as company reconnaissance officer in operations on September 27, near Inchy-en-Artois and September 30 at Sancourt. In the first case the success of the operation was mainly due to his reconnaissance of the Canal du Nord and of the route up to it. He led the company tanks right up to the front line and set each one off in the right direction at zero. In the second case there was no time to make a previous reconnaissance of the ground leading up to the starting-point, but Lieut. Browne led the tanks on an extremely dark night up to the jumping-off point under heavy shell fire. This officer's hard work and ability had a very material effect on the operations.[14]

---

12 TNA,WO339/60279. However, in *The Tank in Action*, p. 321, he claims that his leave was from 'the middle of the month (February) returning in the first days of March.'
13 These were the 'Savage Rabbit' policy and 'Delta scheme' referred to in Chapter 12.
14 Maurice, *Tank Corps Book of Honour*, pp. 202-203.

On 16 October Browne was promoted to acting captain and Battalion RO of the12th Battalion until 16 November but it was not until 5 February 1920 that his rank was made substantive. Operating on a battlescape untouched by the war since 1914, his last action took place north of the River Selle at Beaurain. On 1 November his final act before the Armistice was to route the 12th Battalion back to winter quarters at Curie, north of Arras.

Lieutenant N.M. Dillon saw the first tanks and 'was very intrigued, being mechanically minded, and would have liked a ride in one.'[15] In August 1914 he was a former Haileybury Public School boy training as a mining engineer at Seaham Colliery, Northumbria. Although just eighteen he did not hesitate to volunteer 'when an urgent call was made for Officers or those with OTC training at Public Schools'.[16] He was interviewed at Fenham Barracks, Newcastle and commissioned in the 14th Battalion, Northumberland Fusiliers. Later the Battalion was converted into a Pioneer Battalion. He was not overly impressed with his senior officers nor his early training as 'no heed had been taken of the lessons of the Boer War, and the battlefield tactics were much the same as at Inkerman and other Crimean engagements.'[17] Whilst at Halton Park Camp near Aylesbury Dillon acquired a motor cycle. Motor cycling skills, together with the ability to use a prismatic compass, were valuable assets for a future Tank RO. He embarked for France on 15 September 1915 and arrived at Vermelles and Le Routoire Farm in Reserve during the Battle of Loos. Here he had his first experience of route finding having been ordered to find the way to the Battalion's bivouac location. His experience in digging 'Russian Saps' together with his mining background led to a temporary transfer to 178 Tunnelling Company, Royal Engineers, in time to dig mines under the Tambour near Fricourt for the opening day of the Battle of the Somme on 1 July 1916. Later, close to Delville Wood, Dillon was again able to exercise his route finding skills when ordered to take supplies at night to the front line

> So out came my prismatic compass, and I measured out the bearing and the distance of the first thing we might recognise, which was a farm track. I told my Platoon Sergeant to count how many paces he took, and to tell the men to do likewise in order to keep their interest. I allowed half the usual pace owing to the appalling conditions of mud, etc, and set off following the compass. Sure enough we hit some gravel, and here was the remains of our road.[18]

---

15 BLUL, Record of N. M. Dillon, p. 13.
16 N. M. Dillon, Record of N. M. Dillon (Liddle Collection, University of Leeds, GS 0459, date obscure), p. 1.
17 Ibid., pp. 1-2.
18 Ibid., pp. 12-13.

On a later occasion:

> There were groups of unfortunate soldiers, who had either lost their guide, (or he was lost himself) calling out "Lost again". I suppose I was not much better than others, but at least I had my compass and knew how to use it, and never got lost. My men regarded this as black magic. Nevertheless it gave them confidence.[19]

Some days later Dillon recalled 'our Division was staging an attack, and we were in reserve (again) near the village of Flers. It was a stinking night. The Germans were putting over everything they had … at the same time a queer object came crawling over the mud, and there was IT.! (sic). This was the first tank action.'[20] Later an unhappy change in Commanding Officer motivated him to volunteer for the tanks. 'Here was a chance of doing something useful, and perhaps getting a motor cycle. I don't know if I did much good, but I got my motor cycle, and this was a joy.'[21] Consequently, on Christmas Day 1916, Dillon reported to B Company, 2nd Battalion of the then named Heavy Branch Machine Gun Corps at Pierremont, a village near Bermicourt (see map 5). It was here that he was selected to become one of the new Reconnaissance Officers because, as he claimed, of his map reading skills. Another officer, Capt. Cazalet, became a Reconnaissance Officer because he was apparently gifted with an unerring sense of direction. Captain T. Nelson, a Scottish Publisher, who was killed at Arras, possessed 'granite common sense'.[22]

No archive evidence has come to light to establish the official criteria for selection as an RO. However, it would appear that Tank Corps HQ was guided by Field Service Regulations (Part 1) in focussing on both personal

Norman M. Dillon (later Colonel).

Caption within image: The Memoirs of COLONEL N. M. DILLON *Born 27th July 1896 Died 17th Oct. 1997*

19   Ibid., p. 13.
20   Ibid., p. 13.
21   Ibid., p.14.
22   Beach, 'Scouting for Brigands' in Searle, *Genesis, Employment, Aftermath*, p. 116.

and technical skills (see above). The anecdotal evidence suggests that it was based upon perceived skills and talents, especially in map reading, compass work and graphical skills (the skill of communicating through drawings and other visual means).[23] These skills were mainly acquired in civilian life or demonstrated during training or were a consequence of a natural aptitude for spatial relationships and graphicacy. ROs had to employ the higher order cognitive skills of analysis, synthesis and evaluation in their work.[24] Their intelligence and literacy was not only demonstrated in the quality of their reports but also in their post-war authorships.

'While the General Staff officers on H.Q.s (sic) were almost without exception regulars' the majority of ROs, like the rest of the Tank Corps personnel, were not.[25] 'The whole of the Administrative and Engineering staffs with one solitary exception were drawn from civil occupations.'[26] It has already been noted that Henriques was a 'Social Worker', Dillon a Mining Engineer and William-Ellis an Architect. Douglas Gordon Browne, a Tank Commander and subsequently the author of *The Tank in Action*, was recorded as an Artist on the 1911 Census but by 1914 according to his Attestation Form he was an author.[27] Baker-Carr also records that the unnamed RO of C Battalion, 1st Tank Brigade, was a London lawyer.[28] The Tank Corps clearly 'tapped (into) that great reservoir of urban middle class talent.'[29]

Elles valued the 'idiosyncrasies' which characterized a number of his officers.[30] The new arm seemed to welcome the inventive mind; those 'who were thinking in a novel way as befitted the machines they were there to make of value'.[31] Reference has already been made to Williams-Ellis who created the neologisms 'Reconography' and 'Reconogram'. Consequently, many of the ROs gained for themselves the reputation of being slightly eccentric. Williams-Ellis was described as 'rather arty crafty, and used to walk about with a long stick up to his shoulders shaped like a shepherd's crook'[32] Gibot and Gorczynski commented that ROs had the reputation for being "a little mad".[33]

23 W. G. V. Balchin, 'Graphicacy Should be the Fourth Ace in the Pack', *The Cartographer*, (1966), pp. 23-28. The other 'aces' are Numeracy, Literacy and Oracy; all skills required of a RO.
24 B.S. Bloom, *Taxonomy of Educational Objectives, Handbook I, the Cognitive Domain*, (London, Longman, Green & Co., 1955). For reconnaissance purposes Tank Commanders only used the lower orders of cognitive skills, i.e. knowledge (e.g. of map scales), comprehension (e.g. map reading skills) and application (e.g. the ability to use a map to navigate).
25 Elles quoted in Williams-Ellises, *The Tank Corps*, p. x.
26 Ibid., p. x.
27 TNA, WO339/60279.
28 Baker-Carr, *From Chauffeur to Brigadier*, p.207.
29 Barnett, C. *The Swordbearers*, (London, Cassell & Co.2000 [1963]), p. 180.
30 Ibid., p. x.
31 BLUL, Record of N. M. Dillon, p. 15.
32 Dillon, Ibid., p.15.
33 Gibot & Gorczynski, *Following he Tanks*, p. 78.

Because of their role as trainers and lecturers (see below) they were sometimes called 'Professors'.[34] Baker-Carr noted that at Cambrai 'General Elles, Hotblack, Martel, Williams-Elles and others were able to indulge their predilection for crawling about in unhealthy spots.'[35] 'Therefore it could be argued that, by diversity of background and self-selection, this recruitment pool contained those already disposed towards unorthodoxy and innovation.'[36] Out of this motley crew 'the Reconnaissance Department was organised within the Tank Corps and was, without doubt, the most efficient in the British Army.'[37]

Following the establishment of the Reconnaissance Department in France that drew on existing officers, subsequent appointments came from newly recruited officers in the UK. Both volunteers for the Tank Corps and conscripts undertook reconnaissance training as a part of their initial basic training at Bovington (see below). Recruits who demonstrated an aptitude for reconnaissance work eventually underwent advanced reconnaissance training in France.

Table 1, Appendix II, lists the 74 ROs that have been identified so far. A number of ROs have been detected whilst trawling through the literature on the Tank Corps. Although there are no specific studies of ROs, some authors name them and indicate, in passing, the type of activities in which they were engaged and the difficulties they faced. F.G. Maurice is particularly valuable since he lists those RO officers with their units who received decorations. The citations also describe their activities.[38] They help, together with 'Order of Battle 1918'[39] and those recorded in Tank Corps unit diaries to identify the ROs. The introduction of the reconnaissance specialist into the structure of the Tank Corps was not always a smooth operation.

34   Graphite, *Reconography*, p. 7.
35   Baker-Carr, *From Chauffeur to Brigadier*, p.258.
36   Beach, 'Scouting for Brigands' in Searle, *Genesis, Employment, Aftermath*, p. 117.
37   Baker-Carr, *From Chauffer to Brigadier*, p. 193. This extravagant claim may reflect Baker-Carr's bias but equally he may have a point.
38   Maurice, *Tank Corps Book of Honour*, pp. 71-234.
39   TCMA, the 'Order of Battle' only names the Brigade and Battalion ROs.

8

Growing Pains

The introduction into any organisation of new technology and ideas about its usage can produce unintended consequences for both its formal (organisational) and informal (social) structures. In the BEF it arose from the circumstance that the new technology of the tank was rapidly introduced into the established army organisation which lacked any appropriate doctrine to manage it. This provided a military case study of the circumstances that arise within a 'Socio-Technical System'.[1] This system was first described by Eric Twist of the Tavistock Institute in 1951, but in the totally different context of coal mining. If the BEF displayed the characteristics of such a system consequent upon the progressive introduction of new technology and weaponry, then it might explain why strains occurred to the formal structure and social organisation within both the BEF and the Tank Corps itself.

'Technology' refers here not just to its hardware, the tank, but also to ideas about tank operations (tactics). Whether one accepts that the introduction of the tank constituted another genuine 'Revolution in Military Affairs (RMA)', that is, Armoured Warfare[2] or not, it required the new Tank Corps to examine and adapt traditional reconnaissance organisation and skills to its specific needs. Consequently there was controversy and a temporary cost to the efficiency and success of the Tank Corps' Reconnaissance Branch. At least three tensions arose within the new Reconnaissance Branch. The first was the tension referred to by Dr Jonathan Boff, albeit in a different context which he has described as 'the pragmatic over the programmatic', practice and theory.[3] A second tension was an unintended consequence of the establishment of the

---

1   E. Trist & W. Bamforth, 'Some Social and Psychological Consequences of Long Wall Method of Coal-Getting' in *Human Resources*, Vol.4., pp. 3-38, 1951.
2   Gary Sheffield, *Forgotten Victory* (London, Headline Book Publishing, 2001 [2002]), pp.140-141. It was probably left to Heinz Guderian to institute a RMA with the creation of the Panzer Division and the greater mobility allowed with advances in tank technology.
3   Jonathan Boff, *Winning and Losing on the Western Front*, (Cambridge, Cambridge University Press, 2012), p.249.

ROs as a separate body from unit and tank commanders. The third tension arose from the ROs' responsibilities for both primary and secondary reconnaissance.

The initial *raison d'etre* of the RO was to ensure that the tanks could be brought successfully to the start point for an attack. Yet *Standing Orders* also clearly placed responsibility on the Section Commanders 'for choosing (subject to the approval of the Company Commanders) the routes by which their tanks will move up to the front line'.[4] This created an ambiguity that was fully recognised amongst senior commanders because 'in practice it is the R.O. who selects the routes and tapes them where necessary and although 'the duties of the RO's have been laid down in Standing Orders, (but) they are capable of more precise definition and might be extended in several particulars.'[5]

The author undertaking his own reconnaissance of the 'River' Crinchon. (Bruce Cherry)

4   TCMA, 'HQ: Provisional Standing Orders for Operations, 23 September 1917'.
5   TNA, WO95/104, 'War Experiences, Reconnaissance and Intelligence Duties', p. 9.

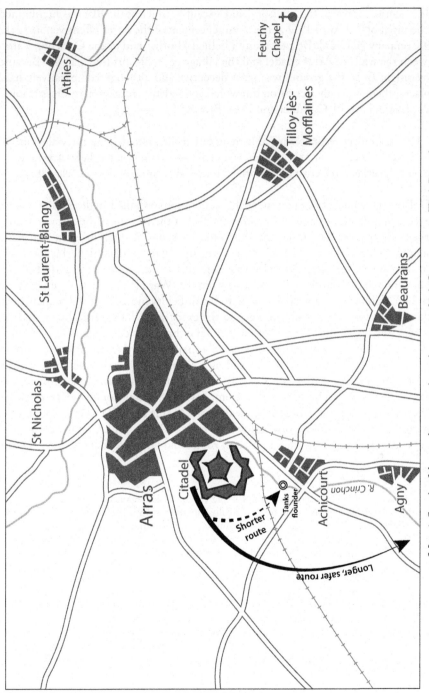

Map 6 South of Arras. A map to show the route of 9th Company, 1st Tank Brigade.

This tension between the 'advisory' and 'executive' roles of the RO was highlighted on the night of 8-9 April 1917 at the commencement of the Arras offensive. Six tanks of 9 Company (1st Tank Brigade) sank ('bellied') in the mud of the Crinchon Valley between the walls of Arras citadel and the village of Achicourt (see map 6).[6] Because of overnight frost 'the ground was most deceptive and although comparatively hard in places, there was only a crust on top which concealed a treacherous morass below.'[7] According to both J.F.C. Fuller and D.G. Browne

> Had the officer reconnoitring this route tested the ground along the valley by pushing a stick into it, this accident would not have occurred, for the stick would have penetrated the crust and informed him of the nature of the soil below it.[8]

D.G. Browne, who was not present at this action, follows Fuller in describing it as an 'inexcusable calamity' that he also laid at the feet of the RO since 'the reconnaissance of the route had been perfunctory... the officer responsible had not even tested the ground with his stick'.[9] On the other hand, the unit diary claimed that 'this route had been carefully reconnoitred and sleepers and brushwood laid over the softest places' but not enough.[10] David Fletcher quoting from the 'War History' of C Company, 3rd Battalion, Tank Corps, adds that 'owing to the difficulty in steering, and to ineffective brakes, it was found impossible to keep to the exact route.[11] The critical issue though was who was responsible for the decision to take this short-cut route of known difficulty 'when a long detour around the head of a shallow valley' (of the River Crinchon) was also available?[12] The decision according to *Standing Orders* ought to have been made by the unit commander since the 'ROs should *only* (emphasis added) be responsible for *indicating* (emphasis added) to Company and Section Commanders which are the best routes available.'[13] Beach draws attention to this dilemma when he quotes the Superintendent of Training, Bovington who indicated that Tank Commanders 'must take great responsibility in the selection of routes and not leave that selection entirely

---

6   One tank that bellied-up here was 'Lusitania' (Second Lieutenant C.F. Weber) which after it was extricated went on to successfully support the 46th Brigade in their attack on 'Railway Triangle'. See P. Barton & J. Banning, *Arras*, [London, Constable, 2010, pp. 134-135]).

7   David Fletcher, *Tanks and Trenches*, (Stroud, Sutton Publishing Ltd, undated), p. 23.

8   Fuller, *Tanks in the Great War*, p. 105.

9   Browne, *The Tank in Action*, p.69. Here he seems to draw on Fuller's, *Tanks in the Great War 1914-18*, p. 105.

10   TNA WO 95/100, 'Narrative of Operations 9th to 11th April 1917, inclusive, SOUTH OF RIVER SCARPE.' This, of course, might be a self-serving entry.

11   Fletcher, *Tanks and Trenches*, p. 23 and TCMA RH86TC 3 Bn., p. 2.

12   Williams-Ellises, *The Tank Corps*, p. 51. William-Ellis was also the battalion intelligence officer with the 1st Battalion at this time.

13   LHMA, 'Summary of Tank Operations, 1st Brigade Heavy Branch', 9th April-3rd May, Appendix I.

to company (ROs)'.[14] Later the confusion was resolved when the decision was clarified about the responsibility for the routes that tanks must follow.

> 'In practice it is the RO. who selects the routes and tapes them where necessary. The responsibility ... should be transferred to the R.O. who should also be made definitely responsible, under the unit Commander ... for the choice of all moves' during operations ... i.e. for routes from detraining point to Tankodrome, from Tankodrome to lying up place before action; from lying up place to point of deployment and from point of deployment to starting point. ... The R.O. should, in short, be responsible that every tank can find its way to its destination'[15]

Perhaps there is an analogy here between the tank commander's responsibility for ensuring his tank arrives safely at the jumping off (starting) point and the RO's responsibility for the route it takes with the captain of a ship who normally follows the directions of a pilot if it is to arrive safely in harbour but will override the pilot if he believes that the pilot is hazarding his vessel.

In the sphere of camouflage there was a similar revision of responsibilities in the light of experience. According to *Standing Orders* tank commanders were responsible for ensuring their tanks were appropriately camouflaged. The tanks carried a net for this purpose. However, it became clear that because of their greater expertise in air photographic interpretation ROs gained a German pilot's eye view of stationary tanks and their lying up places along the prescribed routes. It made sense, therefore, that the ROs, who selected routes and locations, should be responsible for ensuring the tanks would be obscured from aerial observation.

Field Service Regulations, Part 1 together with the creation of a specialist Reconnaissance Branch was the source of a second tension. The Tank Corps clearly took cognisance of the recommendation in *FSR Part 1* to 'carefully revise and keep up to date' *Standing Orders*. It also appointed 'quick and intelligent observers ... possessed of judgement and determination.' The Corps ensured that ROs 'were highly trained' with 'considerable technical knowledge' and 'operating with the best equipment'. Behind the front line they were housed in more substantial Nissen huts where they both messed and worked in contrast to their fellow Tank Commanders in meaner A-frame (Armstrong) canvas billets. The precept was followed that ROs would 'not be unduly restricted in their movements' to the extent they had ready access to motor cycles which they could also unofficially use for social purposes. In practice the veil of secrecy they worked under meant they also had access to privileged information about future operations which, at the time, their Unit and Tank Commanders did not possess. The liaison work they undertook with the Infantry, Artillery and Flying Corps in particular led them to share the company (and dining table) of very senior

---

14   James Beach, 'Scouting for Brigands', in Searle, *Genesis, Employment, Aftermath*, p. 118.
15   TNA, WO 95/104, 'War Experiences, Reconnaissance and Intelligence Duties'.

officers and distinguished personages. At the same time they never had to face life
threatening activities in the field to the same extent as their fellow Tank Commanders.
Dillon suggests that the post of RO was perceived as a 'soft job'.[16] This elitist status
of the ROs concerned Tank Brigade Commanders who felt that they had become 'a
separate caste'[17] who were getting a bit above themselves and needed a 'slap on the
wrist':

> There has been a tendency in the Tank Corps to keep Reconnaissance rather as
> a thing apart. It is difficult to understand this exclusiveness when it is considered
> how very much reconnaissance forms part of the tank scheme of things. Unlike
> every other branch, except perhaps the engineering side, communications with
> regard to reconnaissance have been made direct to the officer concerned and (not)
> through "the usual channels". This practice should be stopped and not allowed
> to creep in again. It has all the grave disadvantages of an *imperium in imperio*
> (emphasis added) without any proportionate compensating value. It sometimes
> results in an anomalous situation as where an R.O. takes action without his C.
> O's (sic) knowledge or approval, on the instruction of some authority other than
> his C.O.[18]

Thus although all unit and tank commanders were trained in reconnaissance work
the ROs' expertise and specialist responsibilities, together with their 'privileges', led
to them emerging as a distinctive caste within the Tank Corps. Beach notes that this
attitude was shared across the whole BEF intelligence scene when he writes that 'the
separate identity of an intelligence "caste" was a source of great unease.'[19]

A third tension occurred as a consequence of the manner in which the ROs were
expected to carry out their duties. It was not long before the RO became the head of
a small reconnaissance team. They were assisted by a Deputy RO, a Draughtsman
and an Orderly. The issue of the delegation of responsibilities arose as it might in
any complex organisation where individuals have multiple tasks. It has already been
shown that Reconography included both primary reconnaissance (field work) and
secondary reconnaissance (map and photograph analysis for example). Brigadier
General Hardress-Lloyd (Fuller's *beau sabreur*),[20] commander of 3rd Tank Brigade,
referred to the latter as 'office work' when he opined that 'Company R.O's (sic) should
be left as far as possible with no office work in their hands, which will keep them from
their main duty, which is to get to know their area and teach it to their Company.' One
suggestion he made was that more office work should be delegated to Battalion ROs.

---

16   TCMA, Dillon Papers, E 2006, 151.3.
17   TNA, WO95/112, '5th Brigade, War Experiences', (undated), also quoted in Beach,
      'Scouting for Brigands', p. 118.
18   TNA, WO95/104, '3rd Brigade, 1 April 1917-31 December 1917, War Experiences', p. 9.
19   Beach, *British Intelligence and the German Army 1914-18*, p.17.
20   Fuller, *Tanks in the Great War*, p. xvi.

But later he expressed the contrary view that the Battalion Reconnaissance Officer should also 'devote a greater amount of his time to outdoor work'.[21] This attitude may well reflect the traditional role of front line reconnaissance operators, for instance the cavalry, who worked in the field 'in contrast to the new wave of "indoor" intelligence work'.[22] This was also recognised in the wider Intelligence scene where an anti-intellectual streak can be detected since 'it would appear that for some there was a crude perception that intelligence collection activities were considered sufficiently active, military and relevant while more sedentary analytical work was not'.[23] However, the RO's expertise was never regarded as unhelpful or 'eyewash' ('I[ntelligence] wash') by their commanders but rested on the knowledge that the ROs had not only to determine tank routes but guide them into battle and follow them on to the battlefield. In modern parlance 'they had to walk the walk, not just 'talk the talk'.

There was never an overarching doctrine of Tank Corps reconnaissance, only a series of activities arising from experience and traditional reconnaissance practices as outlined in FSR (Part 1). It is only with hindsight that a clear pattern emerges which provides a rational framework in which Tank Corps reconnaissance activities may be analysed. In broad terms, Intelligence and Reconnaissance duties between 15 September 1916 and the Armistice (784 days) fall into three principal categories:

(A) Training which occurred in both the UK and France and which was continuous throughout the period of tank operations. In 1917-18 training was undertaken both consecutively and concurrently with other operations depending on circumstances. Establishing training programmes was one of the first actions of the recently appointed HQ staff in November 1916.

It had three essential purposes:

a)   To instruct ROs in advanced reconnaissance skills;
b)   To provide methods and materials necessary to teach Tank and Unit Commanders reconnaissance skills;
c)   To instruct new drafts of Tank and Unit Commanders in more advanced reconnaissance techniques.

B)   Offensive Reconnaissance which included Strategic, Tactical and Battle (Combat) Reconography which engaged the ROs for nearly 80% of their time in active operations.

C)   Protective Reconnaissance (20%) for defensive operations which involved both preparation and operational activities including:
     (a) Defensive reconnaissance;

21   TNA, WO95/104, 3rd Brigade HQ, April-December 1917.
22   Beach, 'Scouting for Brigands', p. 114.
23   Beach, British Intelligence and the German Army 1914-18, p.16.

Reconographic
Cycle (fig, 2).

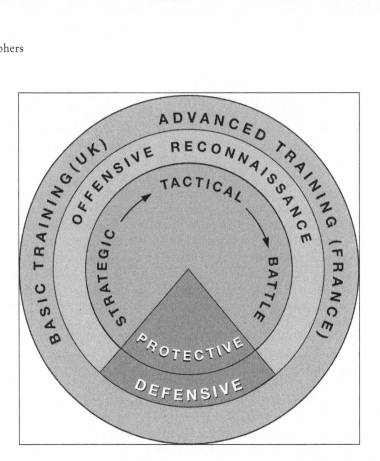

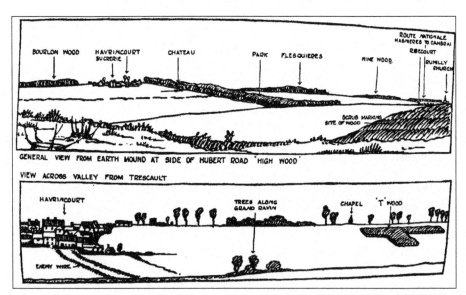

Strategic Reconnaissance of Cambrai. Reconograms drawn by Williams-Ellis. (TCWEF)

(b) Operations with tanks during the retreat caused by the German Spring Offensive in March 1918;

(c) Operations without tanks.

These activities are represented in fig. 2:

A closer examination of offensive reconnaissance shows four phases during the set-piece engagements at Arras (April 1917), Messines (June 1917), Third Ypres (July 1917), Cambrai (November 1917), Hamel (July 1918) and Amiens (August 1918) and the local engagements that followed Amiens in the mobile operations during the 'Hundred Days':[24]

1) strategic or exploratory reconnaissance;
2) tactical or directed reconnaissance which included both primary and secondary information gathering, together with the collection, collation and presentation (graphicacy) of intelligence material as well as liaison with other arms;
3) battle (combat) reconnaissance prior to Y/Z night and during the action on Z day;
4) Post-action activities

The models (fig.2 and fig.3, see page 113) provide the frameworks in which the work of the Intelligence and Reconnaissance officers will now be considered.

---

24   This excludes the tank action and reconnaissance in support of the French at Moreuil.

9

Reconnaissance Training

The 'primitive' tank was a novel, complex machine that needed to be driven, to fight, be maintained and supplied as well as navigated in tactical formations in concert with other arms.[1] All tank activity was concentrated into two years and under wartime conditions whilst fighting a courageous and skilled enemy. This was a major challenge for the Corps which it met through a tailored training system.[2] 'At Bermicourt and at Wool the deficiencies of the old Thetford training were recognised. The experience gained on the Somme had been assimilated. Instructors now knew exactly what they much teach and this time the spirit of the course of training was definite and businesslike.'[3] The importance of organised training was inestimable.

Reconnaissance training followed a system of:

a) Basic training at Bovington (Wool);
b) Tank Corps Training Schools in France at Bermicourt and on the coast at Merlimont and Le Treport;
c) Brigade and Battalion training activities;
d) 'On the job' training.

On 27 October 1916 the Tank Corps base depot moved from Thetford to Wool (Bovington). Basic training for newly commissioned tank officers, which increasingly included conscripted officers, included reconnaissance activities and took place at Bovington and the adjacent camps at Wareham and Swanage under the direction of Brigadier General W. Glasgow.[4] One Tank Commander described a reconnaissance training activity:

---

1   Elles suggests that 'not more than two or three per cent. (of tank crews) were professional soldiers'. Williams-Elleses, *The Tank Corps*, p. x.
2   Fuller, *Tanks in the Great War 1914-18,* p. 164.
3   Williams-Ellises, *The Tank Corps*, p. 40.
4   D.E. Hickey, *Rolling into Action* (Naval & Military Press reprint of 1936 edition), pp. 26-27.

Other interesting courses at Wareham were those on that *most important subject, reconnaissance* (emphasis added). Parties of officers, note book in hand, were sent to make a detailed report on Poole station from the tank point of view. They had to discover whether it were (sic) a junction or a terminus, the type of country each side of the line, the gauge, the number of lines and how they were laid, the type of rail with weight in pounds per square yard, the gradients, the measurements of the platform and the materials of which it was made, the types of signalling, the rolling stock, the number of engines, details of tunnels, cuttings, and embankments; the position and measurement of ramps and their suitability for un-loading of tanks, the conditions of the roads leading to the station, the water supply, the facilities for night entraining, and the position of level crossings, etc. Swarms of officers clambered over the rails and sidings, noting and measuring. Others seriously paced the platforms or stormed the signal-boxes in search of information. The astonished railwaymen gaped at them open mouthed. Had the British Army gone mad? They might have been confirmed in their diagnosis had they seen the results of this mighty investigation on some of the weird scraps of paper which were handed in under the heading of "Plan of Poole Station."[5]

This account gives some idea of the details required for a reconnaissance for a successful entraining and detraining of tanks and should be borne in mind when operational reconnaissance is discussed later. Another Tank Officer in training learned the importance of reconnaissance the hard way. The tank for which he was responsible strayed and sank into marshy ground. He reported that 'this unfortunate episode made a lasting impression on me as to the necessity of testing ground before taking a tank over it, or keeping to the beaten track.'[6] It was also a part of basic training that future tank commanders and ROs learned elementary air photographic interpretation. It was at this stage that potential ROs were identified. Before being given a posting trainee ROs undertook a period of front line observation. Henriques witnessed both the battle of Arras in April and Messines in June 1917 before his posting to 1st Brigade and action during the Third Ypres.[7]

Commanders and crews together with reinforcements received advanced training at the Schools in France under the general direction of Lieutenant Colonel J.F.C. Fuller supported by Major H. Boyd-Rochfort (GSO2 Training).[8] A fundamental 'object of training is to create a "Corps d'Elite".'[9] Fuller based a number of his indoor training schemes on the experiences of Beaumont Hamel and the Ancre area in 1916.[10] The Tank Corps Training Schools were established in order 'to coordinate policy and

5   Mitchell, *Tank Warfare*, pp. 86-87.
6   Hickey, *Rolling into Action*, p. 30.
7   Army Personnel Centre, Glasgow, Army Form B.199, Henriques Military Papers.
8   Post war Boyd-Rochfort became a successful racehorse trainer.
9   Ibid., p.4.
10   Liddell Hart Military Archives, Fuller Papers, 1/1, 20 January 1917.

systems and so to arrive at uniformity of doctrine' and so relieving 'Commanders of their initial responsibility'.[11] They also existed 'for the primary purpose of training Instructors to 'assist Commanding Officers in the training of their units'.[12] The Tank Battalion Reconnaissance Officers' course was of 'twelve working days' and was led by Capt. (Major) F.E. Hotblack (GSO2 Intelligence) and others with reconnaissance experience like Captain (Major) C. Williams-Ellis.[13] It aimed at disseminating experience and good practice. A further purpose was 'to supply Battalion Reconnaissance Officers with the necessary materials for carrying out Courses for their Sections and Tank Commanders within their own units.' The syllabus included:

> (i) Topography of all sectors of British Fronts, characteristics of geology, obstacles and defences of each sector. (ii) Outdoor schemes. Use of the compasses by day and night. (iii) Field sketching, (iv) Simple field engineering for tank routes. (v) Indoor scheme for reconnaissance work of a battle area (from first visit to rapid reconnaissance of new ground after the launching of the first attack). Use for this purpose, of topography, geology, inhabitants' statements, aeroplane photographs, prisoner examination and personal reconnaissance from O.P.s and from the air. Best method of conveying information obtained to other officers of the unit.[14]

N.M. Dillon described his experience of such a course:

> On this course, to attend which we walked some 3 miles, we did exercises in map reading, field sketching, elementary writing of military and orders and so forth. Some of the instruction seemed to be rather imaginative. In field sketching I managed to draw a reasonable picture of a supposedly enemy position from a vantage point, but what good it served I don't know. We never put this artistry into actual practice, but it pleased Williams-Ellis.[15]

RO Instructors were also taught how to lecture by avoiding 'manualese', to speak in parables, use quaint turns of speech or happy colloquialisms, not to drone or bore the listener and be 'neither Preacher nor Stump-orator', to employ epigrams and aphorisms, call for questions and keep the audience's attention by making a deliberate slip. ROs were advised to dash off rough sketches which were more intriguing than

---

11   GS943, *Instructions for the Training of the Tank Corps in France, 1st December, 1917*, p. 3.
12   Ibid., p. 3.
13   Williams-Ellis, *Architect Errant*, p. 128. Williams-Ellis was appointed temporary GSO2 (I) after Hotblack was wounded on 29 September 1918.
14   GS943, p.27.
15   Brotherton Library University of Leeds, Record of N. M. Dillon, p. 15.

prepared diagrams, to use black and coloured chalk on a flip chart and not to stand between the audience and the sketch. Williams-Ellis offered a final piece of advice:

> Remember that your audience consists of human individuals; they are no more sacks of potatoes than you are a gramophone. They will, however, infallibly approximate to the former should you be so ill-advised as to model yourself on the latter. A lecturer has the audience he deserves.[16]

It was the Brigade and Battalion Commanders' primary responsibility to 'train the troops they lead into action. This is a principle which must never be departed from.'[17] Hence Company ROs undertook similar courses to that of the Brigade Intelligence Officers but 'under Brigade arrangements.'[18] These courses could be of five days duration and between four and seven sessions including night activities.[19]

4th Tank Brigade, commanded by Lieutenant Colonel (later Brigadier General) E.B. Hankey, undertook such a course on 14 January 1918.[20] It illustrated how the reconnaissance priorities and the principles of training enunciated by Fuller were carried out. It also demonstrated how training cascaded down the chain of command within the Reconnaissance Branch and the special arrangements that were made for ROs.

The objects of this Course will be:

a)   Not so much to train R.O.s in the technical side of their work, as to give them further practice in various methods and devices for imparting their knowledge and the results of their reconnaissance, in the most concise and profitable forms to the actual Section and Crew Commanders who have to fight the Battle.

b)   To give them the opportunity of hearing the experiences of all R.O.s in the Brigade, their successes and their failures during last years (sic) operations, and to enable them to profit by them.

c)   To provide them with the materials for subsequent courses of instruction for Section and Tank Commanders.

d)   To synchronise as far as possible Reconnaissance methods in the Brigade.

A certain amount of original outdoor work in the form of Tank Reconnaissance scheme on the lines of the latest experiences of the Tank Corps as a whole, will be undertaken during the course.

16   Graphite, *Reconography: Simplified Reconnaissance Sketching*, pp. 4-6. Excellent advice for all teachers and lecturers!
17   GS943, p. 3.
18   Ibid., p. 27.
19   TNA,WO95/118, '6th Brigade Training Centre', Appendix K.
20   TNA WO 95/108, HQ, December 1917-March 1919.

At the conclusion of this course Battalions will arrange Reconnaissance Courses for all Section and Crew Commanders and, if time permits, crew N.C.O.s, to be held under the supervision of the Battalion R.O.s. These courses should be run as Company courses, and should not consist of more than 6 to 8 Officers at a time, owing to the difficulty of the Company R.O. personally supervising the work of a larger number.

The general line of instruction to be adopted at these courses will be arranged with Battalion Reconnaissance Officers by the Brigade Intelligence Officer.

The importance of this branch of training and the influence it will have on future operations cannot be over-emphasised. Battalion Commanders should therefore give Battalion Reconnaissance Officers every facility to carry it out successfully.

Other courses were of a technical nature which also spelt out the duties of ROs. In examining the content of these courses a detailed knowledge is gained of the myriad of factors a RO had to bear in mind when reconnoitring routes. Three principal considerations were outlined:[21]

A. Points as regards suitable ground for routes.
B. Obstacles and ground to be avoided.
C. Limits of Gradients and Obstacles to be surmounted.

In more detail, the first point under A, 'Hard Level Ground which is capable of weight bearing', indicates some of the rule of thumb methods employed. It implies that the weight of a Tank amounts to 20 lbs. per square inch. Before the post-Second World War invention of the 'Penetrometer' for measuring the load bearing capacity of soil,[22] the principal instrument was the RO's own ½" diameter ash walking stick. If the RO could push it into the ground with two hands to a depth of twelve to eighteen inches it indicated that it could bear the weight of a tank. If the RO could push it into the ground to the same depth but with one hand then it would only bear a weight of 10 lbs per square inch. If the ash stick could be thrust into the ground up to the handle then it was capable of carrying 5 lbs or less. Later, as the ROs reconnoitred older battlescapes, the ash stick was useful as an 'obstacle detector' in neglected and overgrown ground. ROs were advised to search for old roads if the route would take the tank through ground that had been heavily shelled. Perhaps learning from the Arras debacle referred to above, the ROs were told that it was preferable to take a safe detour rather than the shortest route. It was emphasised that chalk, gravel and stony ground was a preferred surface.

21   TNA, WO/118, '6 Brigade Training Centre', Appendix K.
22   C.W. Mitchell, *Terrain Evaluation* (Harlow, Longmans, 1991), p. 147.

In total, it listed seventeen different types of obstacles that were to be avoided. The list included shell shattered woods, large and deep ditches and small canals, hills that have to be traversed diagonally which could subject the tank to side slip. Soft, greasy, friable and shell torn ground, very deep and greasy shell holes and narrow (less than 8 ft. wide) tracks between shell holes and dug-outs all must be avoided. Tanks would get stuck in trenches with vertical sides, a width greater than 11 feet and a depth of 6 feet. They should not approach nearer than 20 feet to a communications trench that was parallel to the route. Recalling the problem of Captain Archie Holford Walker's tank (see above) a route should not include a sharp turn. A long and steep gradient (500 yards × 1 in 2) that affected the lubrication of a tank together with any obstacle with a gradient greater than 1 in 2 and a length of 10 yards must be avoided. Shell shattered villages that concealed obstacles were a hazard together with narrow sunken roads that could snag the sponsons. 12 inches of water was the maximum depth with which a tank could cope. A maze of trenches, trench traverses that are between 8 and 10 feet apart and with high parapets should be circumvented.

ROs were instructed as to the precise quantitative character of gradients and obstacles. Thus on dry ground a tank could cope with a gradient of 1 in 1.2; on wet ground it was 1 in 2.5 and saturated ground only 1 in 4. They were warned that optimum ascent of parapets was 6 feet with a descent of between 12 to 15 feet on to flat and firm ground. 10 feet was the maximum width of trenches that tanks could safely cross. Instructors were very precise as to the sort of tree a tank could push over: it should only have a diameter of between 18 inches and 2 feet depending whether it was a fir, ash, willow or oak. Mitchell also records many of these details.[23]

During the winter of 1918 'while the Tank Corps "stood to quarters"' and 'the Tanks were spaced out along a sixty mile front',[24] the RO's became peripatetic instructors. They visited units to undertake 'improvised' practical reconnaissance training of Tank Commanders, those that 'had been dragged untimely from half-finished courses, several were almost fresh from Wool … units and individuals who had lost "school attendance" to make up'. These were in lieu of the five day courses arranged 'under normal conditions'.[25] This is a point where it is useful to emphasize that reconnaissance work was critical for Tank Commanders and not just the province of ROs. Captain D. E. Hickey, a Section Commander (No. 7 Section, 23rd Company, H Battalion) had undertaken his own reconnaissance to locate a lying–up place for his Section when they arrived at the Ypres salient on 4 October 1917.[26] The Tank Commanders' course was very practically orientated. On the first day there was an introductory lecture, chalk layering of maps, map reading and a comparative study of map and country. On the second day 'visualising country from a map using a model was taught followed by

---

23 Mitchell, *Tank Warfare*, pp. 23-24.
24 Williams-Ellises, *The Tank Corps*, p. 133.
25 Ibid., pp. 155-156.
26 Hickey, *Rolling into Action*, pp. 59-63.

panorama sketching (see Chapter 2) and night guiding. Day three was focussed on practical close observation of country on which they had to write a report on which they were questioned. The fourth day was spent visiting a new location of which they had undertaken a map study and so were able to compare the map with reality. There was 'a lecture on obstacles commonly found on approach marches' (see above). This was followed by work with aerial photographs. They were then taken out to undertake night work and to study navigation by the stars. On the final day they returned to the study of aerial photographs both vertical and oblique and compared them to the actual terrain. A final lecture summarised the special points of the course. In the light of these details it is instructive to compare this professional approach with the reconnaissance experience of Henriques' as one of the first Tank Commanders (Chapter 5).

At the same time, Williams-Ellis moved training on from simple instruction to wider reconnaissance education when 'a new type of discourse was evolved, in which the broader aspects of reconnaissance and the study of country were dealt with.'[27] Local history was taught and 'the place of Reconnaissance in the arts of war'. Inter arm co-operation, new theories of artillery and infantry tactics and the effects of poison gas were some of the topics considered. Where it was impossible to provide such courses due to the size and isolation of a unit 'an itinerant instructor would set the exiles with little schemes to carry out.' They were given practical tasks which would reinforce their eye for country.

Informal or 'on the job' training took place at the assembly points and during battle reconnaissance. The ROs had to coach the Tank Officers and NCOs in an understanding of the intelligence materials presented to them and explain and demonstrate its application to the tasks ahead.[28] In preparation for crossing the *Canal de Nord* on 28 September 1918 the Company RO, Lieutenant D.G. Browne, 'collected the tank commanders in a shell hole and reviewed rapidly for the last time the various points that they had to bear in mind in approaching the canal.' Whilst leading a party of Tank Commanders on a preparatory reconnaissance of their route ROs pointed out the relationship between the graphical materials and the reality.

In the 3rd Tank Brigade document 'War Experiences' a shrewd observation was made about the process and a fundamental purpose of reconnaissance training of Tank Commanders.

> If reconnaissance training is properly carried out ... every officer in the company should be able to take the place of the R.O. if he called (sic) upon to do so. The idea should be inculcated that every individual is his own best reconnaissance

---

27   Ibid, p.156. The ROs were taught 'Human Geography' alongside 'Physical Geography' of the landscape.

28   Browne, *The Tank in Action*, pp. 459-460.

officer. If the R.O.'s (sic) have done their work well, they will have trained all the officers of their unit to become Reconnaissance Officers.[29]

The Reconnaissance Department's contribution to Tank Corps' operations, whilst recognized at the time as of considerable importance, was to become only a temporary unit.

29   TNA, WO95/104, 'War Experiences, Reconnaissance and Intelligence Duties', p. 11.

10

Strategic Reconnaissance

Central to their work and the principal *raison d'etre* of the ROs was route finding and guiding. Exploratory or strategic reconnaissance was undertaken sometime well before any action was contemplated whilst tactical reconnaissance occurred nearer the time of the operation. The time allowed to undertake this work varied considerably depending on the circumstance. It could range from weeks before Third Ypres to hours before an operation during the 'Hundred Days'. Battle (Combat) Reconnaissance took place immediately before and during an attack. The model below (figure 3) is an attempt to summarise these activities.

Strategic Reconnaissance was principally concerned with topography, drainage, geology and pedology[1] as well as the enemy's defences. Hotblack and Martel explored the Ypres salient as early as April 1917 prior to both Messines and Third Ypres. Both officers followed up their strategic reconnaissance with 'appreciations' concerning the employment of tanks in the salient. Hotblack coloured maps to indicate the areas that he believed would be a hazard for tanks if extensive artillery barrages destroyed the drainage system. This was to occur later to the Steenbeek at the foot of the Messines Ridge (not to be confused with the Steenbeek at St. Julien, Ypres). In order to keep a check on conditions Hotblack had air photographs taken daily. He worked out the spread of ill-drained areas which he transferred onto 'swamp maps'. 'A copy of each day's "swamp map" was sent to G.H.Q. until we were instructed to discontinue sending them.'[2] There was, however, a degree of ambiguity in the reconnaissance reports. Hotblack's later report of 13 June indicated that in the Fifth Army operational zone 'the area cannot be considered good for the use of the present type of tank, as too much depends on the weather conditions.' However, he also indicated that 'the main ridge and side spurs should be suitable for tank movement except in *unusually*

---

1   The study of soil types.
2   Fuller, J. F. C., *Memoirs of an Unconventional Soldier*, (London, Ivor Nicholson & Watson, 1936), p.144.

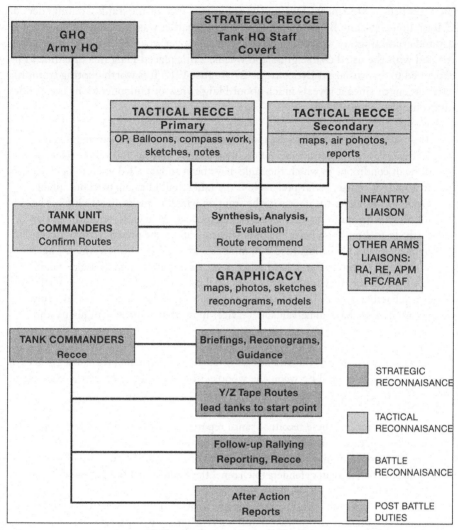

Offensive Reconnaissance (fig. 3).

wet weather.[3] (emphasis added) J.F.C. Fuller, who was very critical of the use of tanks during the Third Ypres Campaign, acknowledges that the reports were not entirely negative. He concedes that a reconnaissance team led by Captain R. C. Knight (B Battalion) and Lieutenant A.E. Scrutton (no. 4 Company) concluded that 'provided a tank kept to its route through the pollard trees, there would be no difficulty in crossing

---

3   Ibid p.133.

the Steenbeek' (Messines).[4] During the reconnaissance of the Tank Commanders of G Battalion (1st Tank Brigade) in July 1917 'the weather was fine, and the surface soil dry and crumbling: we walked, so far as it was safe, over what seemed to be solid earth covered with the usual coarse grass and weeds.'[5] This placed Haig in a dilemma as he explained to Sir Eustace d'Eyncourt on 27 August 1917. It is worth quoting from this letter at length since it reveals much about Haig's view of tank operations even under unfavourable circumstances.

> The conditions favourable to the use of tanks are fully realised here and it is also realised that the present design of the tank cannot show its full value under the difficult conditions in which the tanks have been so far called upon to operate. It would, of course, be far preferable if the tanks could be employed on suitable ground ... however the choice of the front on which to make an attack must be made with regard to many considerations, tactical, strategical, political, and so forth. In making this choice the tank – at any rate in the present state of devel-opment – can only be regarded as a minor factor ... The question which I have to decide, as matters stand, is whether to use or not use the tanks under condi-tions which are unavoidably unfavourable. I have decided that, on the whole, it is advisable to make use of them even under such conditions, and on many occasions they have done valuable service, more than sufficient to justify this decision.[6]

Martel's reconnaissance of the salient east of Ypres had warned of the consequences of tanks having to be routed between the woods either side of the Menin Road beyond Hooge. Hammond opined that

> The importance of these reconnaissance reports cannot be overstated since the single most important factor in the failure of the tank operations that formed part of the opening day of the offensive was not mud but the presence of woods – used by the German defenders to channel the tanks into 'killing grounds'.[7]

Similarly Hotblack and Martel, reconnoitred the Cambrai area weeks before the offensive was sanctioned.[8] It was mentioned earlier how 'General Elles, Hotblack, Martel, Williams-Ellis and others were able to indulge their predilection for crawling

---

4   Ibid, pp. 119-120.
5   Browne, *The Tank in Action*, p. 113.
6   LHMA, Fuller Papers 1/2/12.
7   Bryn Hammond, 'The Theory and Practice of Tank Cooperation with other Arms' (Unpublished thesis, University of Birmingham 2005), p. 147.
8   S. Foot, *Three Lives*, pp. 189-190.

about in unhealthy spots' before Cambrai.[9] Two months prior to the attack Hamel had also been 'carefully reconnoitred.'[10]

During the 'Hundred Days' Somers describe the strategic reconnaissance of the 3 Tank Brigade (Whippet tanks) towards the Hindenburg Line in September 1918 when

> Reconnaissance officers and section commanders commenced a general study and examination of the ground eastwards towards Hargicourt, Villeret and Le Verguier, this area being indicated as a *possible* sector for the Battalion in the *anticipated* (emphases added) operations ... From the 25th to the 29th was a period of preparation and study of the ground in an easterly direction ... Routes, lying-up points, dump sites, refilling points, railway crossings, etc., were all examined, arrangements being made jointly with 9th Tank Battalion, as many portions of the route overlapped and could be used mutually. A suitable lying-up point was selected in the valley west of Grand Priol Woods, and routes from this point eastwards towards the St. Quentin Canal, examined and checked.[11]

Covert Reconnaissance and Deception both strategic and later tactical reconnaissance was undertaken in order to ensure secrecy and both mislead the enemy and indeed the local British infantry units. In January 1917 exploratory (strategic) reconnaissance was made in the Arras area in anticipation of a future offensive.[12] The work was frustrated by the Germans' unanticipated withdrawal to the Hindenburg line.[13] On 6 May 1917, according to the War Diary of the 2nd Tank Brigade, Lieutenant D.M.Dillon was wounded whilst undertaking a reconnaissance. In his memoir a memory lapse on his part occurred when he placed the reconnaissance in February when he was sent to do an inspection of the enemy area near Lens.

> There was an idea of staging an attack there. I had a draughtsman with me, and we went up into various observation points, pit-head gear ... and made numerous sketches. This was a quiet area and, as a rule, one could move about in the open, if in ones or twos. Unfortunately some enemy gunner wanted a target and had a crack at us. I got a piece of aluminium nose-cap in my cheek, and my draughtsman had some in his tongue. As it happened, we were outside the local battalion dressing station, and were soon bandaged and sent to the Casualty Clearing Station, and thence by train to Boulogne, and so to London.[14]

9   Baker-Carr, *From Chauffer to Brigadier*, p. 258.
10   Williams-Ellises, *The Tank Corps*, p. 181.
11   Somers, *The Sixth Battalion*, pp. 168-169.
12   TNA, WO158/137. E. Charteris' *Account of the Battle of Arras*.
13   Baker-Carr, *From Chauffeur to Brigadier*, p. 217.
14   BLUL, Record of D.M.Dillon, p. 16.

No attack took place in the Lens area but was directed at the Messines Ridge.[15] Consequently Dillon missed the action there. This reconnaissance, unbeknown to Dillon, may well have been a ruse. There is no indication that Dillon made any effort to disguise his intention either to the British or the enemy (see below). On 5 June 1917, two days before the Messines operation, and with the same intention of confusing the enemy, two Sections of Tanks were sent to make a demonstration in daylight in the Arras area, between Croiselles and Henin-sur-Cojeul. The expectation was that they would be observed by German aircraft and so 'mislead the enemy into believing that an offensive would take place in that neighbourhood' rather than Messines.[16]

A similar deception (*ruse de guerre*) was used in July 1918 before the Battle of Amiens when ROs were directed to undertake an observable reconnaissance of the areas around Arras and then Gommecourt although there was no intention of launching an offensive in these places when

> Parties of officers were taken up by motor lorry daily to observation points, where they would stand, map in hand, peering through their field-glasses at German positions, while a reconnaissance officer explained the features of the countryside at great length ... Numerous tanks began to appear in the neighbourhood, nestling under the shelter of banks, covered only by their tarpaulins (when) they could (have) been hidden in the woods which were plentiful in this district ... Then ... we were going further south near Gommecourt. The reconnaissance officers set off on their motor bicycles, thoroughly explored the new region, and mapped out routes from the new railhead. At the eleventh hour, however, the plans were suddenly changed once more and the tanks moved across country to a different railhead ... (they) were all part of a clever scheme to mislead the Germans.[17]

It appeared that the 'tanks' that were covered with tarpaulins were actually dummies. Earlier, prior to the Cambrai offensive:

> Every effort was made to disguise the possibility of a tank attack in the Cambrai area. To this end, all badges were removed, all coming and going in the forward area was managed as inconspicuously as possible and plausible explanations and aliases were provided. Here some reconnaissance had already been carried out in the area by Hotblack and Martel, disguised (so the rumour ran) in beards and bowler hats as War Correspondent and Labour Member respectively.[18]

15   TNA, WO95/101, 2nd Brigade War Diary, 9 May, 1917.
16   Somers, *The War History of the Sixth Tank Battalion*, p. 13.
17   Mitchell, *Tank Warfare*, pp. 215-16.
18   Foot, *Three Lives*, p. 190.

ROs removed all badges, buttons and dress that would indicate both to the enemy and their own infantry that tanks might operate in that area.[19] The ROs posed as 'Signals Officers or Trench Mortar Specialists in order to avoid attracting attention among the troops occupying the trenches.'[20] Alternatively, they impersonated Royal Engineer Officers. 'Cock and bull' stories were constructed which even misled other ROs. Before the battle of Amiens, south of the River Somme, there was:

> ... one occasion Major Hotblack and another British Officer met on the banks of the Luce and each made lengthy explanations which explained everything except the real reason they were there. Two days later these officers met at a conference on the operations, and congratulated each other on the plausibility of their several explanations. It had been no easy matter to pretend that it was quite a normal thing for them to paddle in the Luce in close proximity to the enemy.'[21]

It was here that Major-General H. Elles recorded that 'Lieutenant (Temporary Major) F.E. Hotblack, DSO, MC., Norfolk Regiment ... has continued to render very valuable service. Notably – during the recent operations on the SOMME the successful crossing of the LUCE River by Tanks under the very nose of the enemy was chiefly due to the detailed reconnaissance and arrangements made with the French on our immediate right by this officer.'[22]

Behind the front lines at 1st Tank Brigade HQ at Arras a 'double bluff' deception was used to mislead the curious before the Cambrai operation. In an unlocked room 'were ostentatiously hung spoof maps of other topical districts and a profusion of plans lay about.' On the door was a 'No Admittance' notice. The hope was that the insatiable curiosity of 'unauthorised persons' would tempt people to ignore it and ransack the room and so spread false rumours.[23] Before Cambrai the forward Tank Corps HQ at Albert was advertised only as a Training Office. More significantly for the Tank Corps itself the ROs, as mentioned earlier, were party to restricted information about a future offensive that was often denied to their Unit Commanders and other Tank Officers. Brigade Commanders instructed them to undertake reconnaissance covertly. This, as has been noted, helped to set the ROs apart and gave them an advantage denied both to their immediate superiors and the fighting Tank Commanders.

19   Browne, *The Tank in Action*, p. 268.
20   Foot, *Three Lives*, p. 190.
21   Williams-Ellises, *The Tank Corps*, p.195.
22   Letter from Elles to GHQ 25 August 1918 (Army Personnel Centre, Hotblack papers).
23   Ibid., p. 107.

The location by GHQ of a 'set-piece' offensive was communicated down the chain of command as far as Tank Brigade HQs. It was they, through their Brigade Intelligence Officers, who directed Battalion and Company ROs to undertake detailed (tactical) reconnaissance sometimes three weeks beforehand.[24] The 4th Tank Brigade had only six days though to reconnoitre before Amiens which caused the ROs to hurry.[25]

24   TNA, WO 95/100, 1st Brigade war Diary.
25   TNA, WO95/108, '4th Tank Brigade: Report on Operations, August 8-11 1918'.

11

Preparatory Reconnaissance: Tactical

Figure 3 indicates the phases of Tactical Reconnaissance: the primary phase which involves information collection through *first-hand* observation of the topography (visual reconnaissance); the secondary phase in which data is assembled through the interpretation of the topography through *second-hand* data, for example, maps, air photographs, reports. The information gained in both phases is then subject to the third activity: the intelligence *process* of synthesis, analysis and evaluation. The ROs then used their *graphical* skills to render their recommendations for tank routes communicable to Unit Commanders for their approval. Following agreement on routes the RO *liaised* with the other arms involved in the proposed offensive.

Tactical (primary and secondary) Reconnaissance: it is in this phase that the differentiation in reconnaissance responsibilities between the Tank Reconnaissance Department and its fighting units needs clarification. Tank Corps HQ document GS943 outlined their duties ('on which training will be based').[1] All echelons down from Brigade Commanders had a responsibility for reconnaissance. A Tank Officer's duties included 'Reconnaissance of the route of his Tank for its march to the starting point'. The duties of the Battalion and Company ROs were reduced to five lines and appear limited to 'the collection and dissemination of all information' and 'detailed work on maps and aeroplane photographs'. All Unit War Diaries for 1917 clearly show that in fact the ROs had considerably greater responsibilities. This apparent ambiguity is resolved if it is recognized that the fighting tank officers' reconnaissance responsibilities *followed on* from the 'pathfinder' field and office work undertaken by their Unit ROs.

The ROs disappeared from their Units usually on motor cycles ('abominable machines')[2] with side cars (staff cars, horses and legwork were also used from time to

---

1   GS943, *Instructions for the Training of the Tank Corps in France*, (Headquarters Tank Corps, 1st December, 1917), pp. 6-9.
2   'Browne, *The Tank in Action*', p. 325.

time) to undertake the initial 'minute reconnaissance'.[3] Later they would be accompanied by a Draughtsman and/or an Orderly (Servant). When they were mobile the ROs had to contend with road hazards and shellfire.[4] It did, however, provide a degree of independence and privilege that helped to set them apart from other tank officers. Dillon confessed that he took advantage of his access to a motorbike to acquire comestibles for the Battalion's RO mess.[5] When there was little for him to do Browne 'paid the usual visits to Hesdin and 'visited once or twice the field of Agincourt'.[6]

The first task was to determine routes from the 'Detraining Point to our Front line' and eventually 'submitting the routes selected to Company and Battalion Commanders (Heavy Branch) and to the Corps and Divisions concerned'.[7] There is no indication that these routes ever met with disapproval, indeed quite the reverse.[8] There were sometimes objections from the other arms when they feared the tanks would draw enemy artillery fire, damage pipelines, telephone wires or compete with them for road space.[9] The routes selected, (the 'approach march'), generally had four sections: (i) railhead to places of assembly (the 'tankodrome'); (ii) tankodromes to places of deployment (usually by Z minus 1 day), (iii) thence during Y-Z night to the frontline 'start' or 'jumping off' point and (iv) attack routes and objectives:

(i)	(ii)	(iii)	(iv)	
railhead	tankodrome	deployment	frontline	no man's land
● ➡	● ➡	● ➡	● ➡	

All movements took place at night which presented its own challenges.

At the Battle of Messines 2nd Tank Brigade's B Battalion's Approach March was from the railhead at 'Clapham Junction' (vicinity of Dranoutre) to the tankodrome (on X Day) at Gites Camp, near Zwartenmolemhoek, to various assembly points for Y day (Keepaway Farm, a point one thousand yards north-west of Wulverghem and between Stinking and La Plus Douvre farms) to the jumping off points between two and three hundred yards behind the Front Line ready for Z Day. The Approach March for G Battalion, 1st Tank Brigade before Third Ypres commenced at the railhead/tankodrome at Oosthoek Wood from there to the assembly points at Halfway House (see map 7) before crossing the Yser Canal to La Brique (Frascati Farm) for X Day to the jumping off point at Forward Cottage for the attack on St Julien.

3   Fuller, *Tanks in the Great War 1914-18*, p. 59.
4   TNA, WO95/104, 'Report on 3rd Brigade Tank Corps. Operations with the Third Army, November 20th – November 27th'.
5   IWM, Recorded Interview, 8752, 1987.
6   Browne, *The Tank in Action*, p. 381.
7   TNA, WO95/101, '2nd Brigade War Diary, Appendix A, February to December 1917'.
8   The exception, of course, was at Arras and the crossing of the Crinchon valley.
9   BLUL, Record of N.M. Dillon, p. 25.

Map 7 Original plan of the
Halfway House (an assembly
point). (TNA)

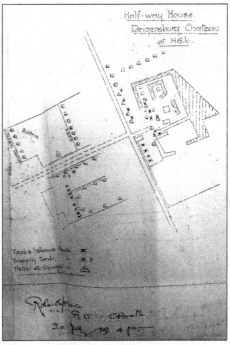

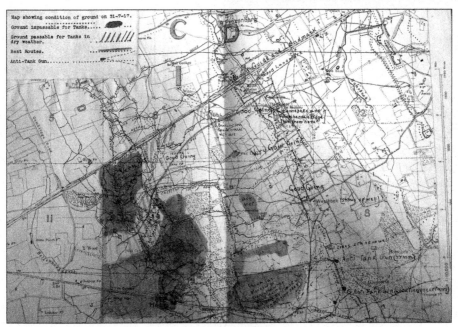

Map 8 An original map of tank 'going' near Frezenberg, July 1917. (TNA)

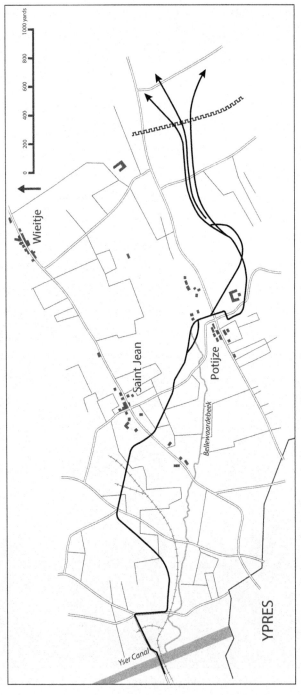

Map 9 Original map for the approach march of C Battalion, Third Ypres. (TNA)

At Cambrai B Brigade's Approach March was from the railhead at Sorel to the tankodome in Dessart (Essart) Wood before assembling near Villers Plouich. The 6th Tank Battalion (3rd Tank Brigade) detrained at Heudicourt, their railhead, before undertaking their Approach March to their assembly point at Gouzeaucourt. On Y/Z night they followed the routed taped by the RO to their jumping off point. In determining the routes for the Approach March the ROs were the 'eyes' of the tanks and used observation posts (OPs), map and air photographs as well as reports (from prisoners and refugees) to make their choice. The application of sketching taught them to analyse the battlescape across no man's land.[10] They would also work out a compass traverse between landmarks when the tanks had to cross a featureless terrain. They also had the benefit of their own ground tests,[11] observations, notes, sketch maps, profile sections and sketches.[12]

The use of kite balloons was less successful. In preparation for tank operations at the Third Ypres, Second Lieutenant E.C.H Shillaker, RO of 3 Company, 2 Tank Brigade, on 14 July 1917, ascended in a balloon belonging to 'No.18 Kite Balloon Section (KBS)' His report was rather negative. 'The visibility was not good … one could not see beyond BROODSEINDE CROSS ROADS with any success and the N. end of the WESTHOEK RIDGE was very indistinct it being absolutely impossible to pick up SOUTH STATION BUILDINGS AND KIT & KAT'.[13] He added that it was no better than looking at a plasticine model and therefore an RO would not gain a great deal. He went on to recommend that balloon observations would be more useful to Tank Commanders after 'their routes had been settled'. However, it seems that the artillery had first call on balloon reconnaissance. 'It was impossible to get the tank commanders up in the last show (Messines) as 18 KBS had a large number of (artillery) shoots to work off and had very little time to devote to anything else.'

The fact that tank movements had to be done at night is an important consideration. *En route* the ROs had to note and test natural and man-made obstacles for tanks, e.g. soft and shell-pitted ground, weak bridges.[14] Equally they had to determine places where the tanks would create problems for other arms, for instance, traffic pinch points, signal wires, pipe lines and narrow-gauge railway lines that crossed the approach march. Supply dumps needed to be located as well as 'half-way' rest stops and arrangements for camouflage. The details were set out in the 6th Tank Brigade's Training Centre document in considerable detail (see chapter 9). It indicated that the start points 'should not be further than 400 yards from the German front line' and advised that the best places to conceal the tanks were old defences but not roads,

10   Graphite, *Reconography*', pp. 12-45. Dillon claims he never used them in the field (BLUL. Record of D. M. Dillon. p. 15).
11   Prodding the ground with their ashplant sticks.
12   Graphite, *Reconography*, p. 20. Williams-Ellis used a telescope to view and sketch landmarks since it could be attached to an ash stick (see Appendix C).
13   TNA, WO95/101, 'Reconnaissance Operations Reports of the 2nd Brigade', 31 July, 1917.
14   TNA, WO95/118, 'Some Notes on Reconnaissance for Tank Routes'.

landmarks and trench junctions. 'Rallying points' for the tanks on the battlefield were also selected. These locations, it was advised, must not be in view of the enemy but in clear sight of the (wireless) Transmitting Station (also selected by the RO) and be of easy access for Supply Tanks but not be in positions used for artillery. It made clear that the ROs had to determine the 'general topography of the area behind the enemy's lines...the enemy's system of defence' as well as 'our system of defence'.[15]

Behind the enemy lines the ROs had to note particularly the 'heavy shelled areas; steep natural banks; road and railway embankments & cuttings; marshy ground; ravines; streams; ditches; bridges (width and strength) and type of soil'. It was important to determine if there were special tank defences including light guns, land mines[16] and tank traps. More generally the ROs had to determine the siting and nature of the enemy trenches and artillery positions including their observation posts (OPs) together with machine gun (MG) and trench mortar (TM) emplacements. They also had to try to locate enemy headquarters and supply dumps as well as wire which might be difficult for the artillery to cut, dug-outs and the 'employment of gas'. The infantry units with which the tanks were to work would supply details of the British system of defence.

Secondary tactical information was collected including maps[17] and intelligence updates from infantry Intelligence Officers and those with whom the tanks were to operate. They acquired a copy of the artillery's fire plan. Increasingly air reconnaissance reports and photographs (vertical and particularly oblique,) made a significant contribution to Tank Corps intelligence. Dillon cited the occasion during the Third Ypres campaign on 27 August:

> ... my section reached a point near Inverness Copse, where it had to debauch across country, and here the going was not too bad. I had planned this route by study of aeroplane (sic) photographs, and by seeing from the map that the contours revealed a slight rise, and therefore less muddy.[18]

As important as this 'office work' was senior commanders had a point in promoting the greater importance of primary reconnaissance. Most secondary sources are at best an approximation of reality. Maps become outdated, contour intervals and form lines mislead as to gradients. Streams depicted on maps give no indication of width, depth or speed of flow especially if they are in spate or if the drainage pattern has been disrupted by an artillery barrage. Land and air photographs have their own vertical and horizontal distortions. Reports of information obtained through the interrogation

---

15   TNA, WO95/118, '6th Brigade Training Centre, 1 January 1917-30 November 1919'.
16   This they failed to do this prior to the attack across the Bellicourt tunnel when twelve tanks ran into an old British mine field sowed by Fifth Army, 16th Division, close to Quennemont Farm.
17   Principally 1/10000 scale.
18   Dillon, p. 19.

of prisoners or refugees reflect the questions asked which may be of little relevance to the Tank RO. It was necessary, therefore, to both 'triangulate' information from these secondary sources and confirm them with primary observation where possible. Circumstances (time and opportunity) would dictate whether it was expedient to begin this work before undertaking primary reconnaissance.

The Intelligence Process: The ROs collated, and synthesised all the information gathered through primary and secondary reconnaissance. The next step was to subject all the information to analysis and evaluation before routes were determined. Michael Occleshaw comments that

> … until all the material extracted from prisoners, documents, aerial observation, patrols, wireless and the other sources covered has been weighed and categorized by the Intelligence Staffs it is merely information, not Intelligence. The **process** (emphasis added) of weighing and cross checking is known as evaluation, a process which very few senior officers were engaged … In essence evaluation is a matter of judgement and sense of proportion. It enables sound decisions to be made which will achieve given ends in the most economical manner in relation to observed facts.'[19]

The detailed recommendations were usually prepared in graphical form for acceptance by the Unit and Tank Commanders so that information could easily be digested and taken into battle. Liaison with other arms was an important element in the intelligence picture.

Liaison: it follows that reconnaissance work had to include considerable cooperation with other arms.[20] The ROs often needed to request practical help besides information from other arms. Royal Engineers would be requested to strengthen weak bridges and fill in particularly large shell holes and old trenches on the tank route. The RFC/RAF was asked to undertake further photographic sorties. Provost Marshals (APM) and all the units through which the Tanks would pass or cooperate had to be alerted to Tank Corps' plans. Central to this liaison work were relations with the infantry units the tanks were supporting. Knowledge of cooperating arms meant that the ROs were well placed to conduct mutual 'public relations' activities, especially with the Australian's following their loss of confidence in the tanks after Bullecourt. Before Amiens

---

19   Michael Occleshaw, *Armour Against Fate. British Military Intelligence in the First World War*, (London, Columbus Books Ltd.,1989), p. 354.
20   Hammond, 'The Theory and Practice of Tank Cooperation with Other Arms on the Wester Front during the First World War' (Unpublished thesis, University of Birmingham, 2005).

To improve relations and mutual understanding, we had parties with our Australian allies, at which they knew no limits. Our camp in the wood was surrounded by a Tank tape, to avoid vehicles, &c (sic) messing up our layout. On the morning after one party, two of our guests were found still following the tape round and round our camp on hands and knees. They thought it was the way home.[21]

The development of 'mutual trust' was paramount. More seriously officers of all ranks messed together, exchanged visits and experienced each other's weaponry. It assisted in mutual understanding, cooperation and confidence. 'Tank personnel and infantry practised together and talked together, and for the first time was reached an approximation to that mutual trust and understanding which these two arms had so long and so especially required.'[22]

Brigade and Battalion Intelligence and Reconnaissance Officers frequently accompanied their senior commanders to Infantry HQs for liaison and planning meetings with Generals.[23] A case in point was during Third Ypres when a proposal came from the 1st Tank Brigade's Intelligence Officer, Williams-Ellis, and was taken to Lieutenant-General Ivor Maxse by Brigadier General C.D'A.B.S. Baker-Carr. This led to the successful Cockcroft operation near St Julien on 18 August 1917 (see above).[24] However, liaison work with the infantry was not always this successful.[25]

The unrealistic expectations of the tanks during their baptism were often still held by the infantry. They never completely withered away in spite of SS164 and SS204.[26] Browne cited the occasion in September 1918 when the infantry Brigadier requested 'two Tanks to mop up after his infantry' and

> ... the scheme did not commend itself to us in the very least. It showed the common misapprehension of the correct use of tanks, and violated all our tactical principles based on bitter experience. There were only two tanks to be used, which left no margin for accidents; they were to be employed wrongly to mop up after the infantry, instead of preceding the latter; the attack was to begin in

---

21   BLUL, Record of D.M.Dillon, pp. 24-25.
22   Browne, *The Tank in Action*, p. 273.
23   Henriques, *Indiscretions of a Warden*, p. 124.
24   TNA, WO95/100, '1st Brigade War Diary, G Battalion Tank Corps, Report on Operations, 19 August 1917', pp. 190-195, Williams-Ellises, *The Tank Corps*, pp. 91-93 and Browne, D.G. *The Tank in Action*, pp. 205-240. Both authors participated in the small but significant operation. They believed it also served to remind the infantry of the potential value of the tanks.
25   Browne, *The Tank in Action*, pp. 485-488.
26   SS164: *Notes on the Use of Tanks and the general principles of their employment as an adjunct to the Infantry attack* (1917). SS204: *Infantry and Tank Co-operation and Training* (March 1918) and TNA, WO 158/832, 'Tanks and their Employment and Co-operation with Other Arms (August 1918)'.

broad daylight; the approach-march necessarily led over the bare and prominent ridge in front of Bapaume, where the machines would be detected before they got into action at all.'[27]

It was sensible that after all this was pointed out to the Brigadier the request was withdrawn.

The ROs' practical knowledge of the ground over which an offensive might be conducted was valuable for the contribution their commanding officer could make to discussions with the infantry. Increasingly Battalion ROs found themselves acting in a Staff (Tactical) role.[28] Dillon described this role as that of an 'assistant tactical officer'.[29] Such meetings with senior infantry commanders usually included an invitation to dine. In extreme instances lowly captains could find themselves at table with royalty. Henriques, perhaps facetiously in a letter to his wife, reported:

> The Generals asked me to meals and we chatted away like pals, and I do rather enjoy it. At the pow-wow there were six generals and eight 'brass hats' and two majors and your humble self ... last night ...I was dining with a major-general (sic) and the Corps Commander...The day before I was with Prince Arthur of Connaught...had tea with a brigadier and then a second tea with a major-general, ending up at the Flying Squadron.[30]

Williams-Ellis also rubbed shoulders with Prince Arthur.[31] Few tank commanders were so privileged. Dillon, however, when he accompanied Lieutenant Colonel E.D. Bryce, his Battalion Commanding Officer, had a less pleasant meal with Major-General George Montague Harper before Cambrai. 'From the start "uncle" Harper was rude and offensive. He said his division would gain its objectives without any b..... tanks. We departed without much useful contact having been made.'[32] There is a mystery here. Lieutenant Colonel Bryce and Captain Dillon belonged to B Tank Battalion which was tasked to support the 6th Division on the opening day of the Battle of Cambrai. Harper's 51st Division was to be supported by D Tank Battalion (CO, Lieutenant Colonel W.F.R. Kyngdon).[33] It is possible that Dillon had 'sour grapes' for lunch since Harper's 51st Division's attack on Flesquières was in the event the least successful of the tank actions at Cambrai.

---

27   Ibid., p. 411. See also Hammond, 'The Theory and Practice of Tank Cooperation with Other Arms on the Western Front During the First World War', p. 343.

28   Williams-Ellis, *Architect Errant*, Ibid., p. 131.

29   Dillon, *Record*, p. 15.

30   L.L. Loewe, *Basil Henriques: A Portrait*, (London, Routledge & Kegan Paul, 1976), p. 52.

31   Williams-Ellis, *Architect Errant*, p. 131.

32   BLUL, Record of N. M. Dillon, p. 21.

33   Gibot & Gorczynski, *Follow the Tanks*, p. 44.

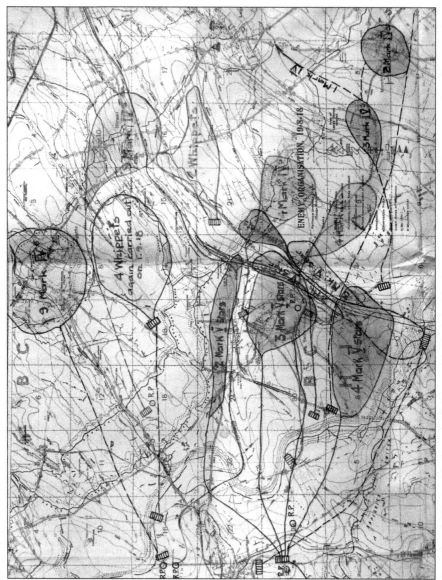

Map 10 An original RO map of tank operations between Bapaume and Arras 1918. (TNA)

CONVENTIONAL SIGNS.

TANK - - - - - - - - - - - - - - - - - - -

STARTING POINT - - - - - - - - - - - - -   S. P.

RALLYING POINT - - - - - - - - - - - - -   R. P.

CAMPS (Word CAMP to be added) - - - - - -

     (other than Tank Units)

MARSHY GROUND - - - - - - - - - - - - -

CUTTING OR EMBANKMENT - - - - - - - - -
(Considered an obstacle)

AIRLINE - - - - - - - - - - - - - - - -

HEAVY SHELLED GROUND - - - - - - - - -
(Considered an obstacle)

HEADQUARTERS BRIGADE - - - - - - - ; - -

UNITS   ⬤ BATTALIONS

          ✕ COMPANY (when detached)

TANK PARK - - - - - - - - - - - - - - -

ASSEMBLY PLACE - - - - - - - - - - -

TRANSPORT PARK - - - - - - - - - - - -

SUPPLY DUMP - - - - - - (existing) - - -

SUPPLY DUMP - - - - - - (suitable site)-

ROUTES - - - - - - - - - - - - - - - -

DETRAINING RAMP - - - - - - - - - - - -

CROSSINGS - - - - - - - - - - - - - - -

WOOD (STANDING) - - - - - - - - - - - -

Conventional signs used on RO's maps. (TCMA)

Graphical Work: rendering all this information manageable drew on the graphical skills of the ROs and their Draughtsmen.[34] Before Third Ypres the Battalion ROs worked together in joint accommodation in the dry and relative comfort of Nissen huts in the grounds of Lovie Chateau (Fifth Army HQ). It allowed them to undertake their work under favourable conditions. Even during mobile operations in 1918 the RO had the benefit of 'a night in a camp bed, followed by a bath and a comfortable breakfast (which) worked wonders'.[35] It has already been mentioned that Dillon hinted that being an RO was perceived as being a 'soft job'.[36]

The graphical work was often of the very highest quality. Annotated coloured maps of the terrain, the approach routes, tank parks and areas of tank exploitation are commendable.[37] The maps that were principally used were at a scale of 1:10,000. The ROs annotated the maps with their own special conventional signs. Landscape sketches could be a positive work of art although it was not the intention. Air photograph mosaics were constructed and tank obstacles were registered on them. Compass traverses were produced to guide Tank Commanders.[38] The landscape could also be modelled in plasticine.[39] The two dimensional map and photograph could then be related to the three dimensional model. The completed graphics were duplicated and issued to Commanders for the next Battle (Combat) Reconnaissance stage either to take with them on a further conducted reconnaissance or to work on beforehand under the supervision of the RO. A useful exercise for the Tank Officer was to 'colour layer' maps between contours in order to impress upon them the variations in the topography they would be traversing.[40] This, however, could be time consuming and consequently sometimes delegated to the RO or more usually his Draughtsman.[41]

By this stage the ROs would have supplied the Tank Commanders with materials including prepared maps and annotated air photographs that would allow them to relate this graphical information to the real ground. In this way misconceptions could be avoided especially when translations of French topographical features could mislead. The 'Grand Ravin' at Cambrai, for instance, was not the deep ravine anticipated. The French word for 'ravine' is 'ravine'! A 'ravin' is an open although relatively steep-sided valley. Henriques also misled the reader in describing the upper section

---

34   TNA, WO95/101, 'Reports of Company Reconnaissance Officers'. They were all in agreement as to the benefits of appointing competent Draughtsmen to compensate for their own limitations in time and skills.
35   Browne, *The Tank in Action*, p. 404.
36   TCMA, Dillon Papers, E2006.1513.
37   See appendices D & E.
38   Williams-Ellises, *The Tank Corps*, p. 79.
39   TNA, WO 95/101, 'Reconnaissance Officers' Messines post action reports'.
40   Sometimes referred to as 'contour shading' that occurred on the 'Bartholemew's Half-Inch series, with its coloured layering of contours' and which the War Office preferred to the Ordnance Survey map. See M. Parker, *Map Addict* (London, HarperCollins, 2009), p. 113.
41   TNA, WO 95/104, 'Report on 3rd Brigade Tank Corps. Operations with the Third Army, November 20th – November 27th'.

of the Wedge Wood-Angle Wood valley north of Maurepas as a 'sort of ravine.' (See the earlier map)[42] This particularly occurs when 'form lines' are drawn between the contours so giving an exaggerated impression of the gradients. The aim was to familiarise the Tank Commanders with the routes and so ensure their safe arrival at the start point on Y/Z night. The final preparation was neatly summarised in the 'after action' report following Cambrai: 'in view of the short time available for topographic coaching for Tank Commanders all material was, as far as possible, prepared for and presented to them in a well sifted, concentrated and pre-digested form. Included in such matters were panoramic sketches and a diagrammatic skeleton map of the Battle area – every Tank Commander received a copy of each.'[43]

---

42   Henriques, *Indiscretions of a Warden*, p. 117.
43   TNA, 95/100 1st Brigade, 7th Battalion War Diary, appendix A.

12

Battle (Combat) Reconnaissance

Battle (Combat) Reconnaissance[1] usually commenced no later than two days before a set piece attack and continued until the tanks were withdrawn from the battle (Figure 3). It took place after the proposed routes to the front line were approved by unit commanders. At this stage the Battalion and Company ROs briefed their senior officers and the Unit and Tank Commanders and issued them with the appropriate maps and 'reconograms'. They then escorted and talked them through the proposed routes ('walk and talk') and to Observation Posts (OPs).[2] This was the point where tank officers' own reconnaissance training was pertinent. The tank commanders were also encouraged afterwards to undertake their own independent reconnaissance as often as time allowed, preferably at least three times. At the start of the Third Ypres operation:

> ... the R.O.s, by means of vertical and oblique aeroplane photographs, pointed out and drilled into the crew commanders and N.C.O.'s the places they would have to clear up on the day they would have to go over the top. After this journeys were made to the front line and advantageous points where peeps over the parapet were taken at such places as Bosart Farm, Pommern Redoubt, Somme Farm and Kansas Cross.[3]

The second stage usually took place two nights before the attack (X/Y Night) whilst stage three occupied the following night (Y/Z), the night prior to the attack. The penultimate activity commenced with the onset of the attack on Z Day. After the action reports had to be written.

1 An alternative description is 'Combat Reconnaissance'.
2 Williams-Ellises, *The Tank Corps*, p.51.
3 Somers, *The Sixth Tank Battalion*, pp. 22-23.

RO guidance
markers. (TCMA)

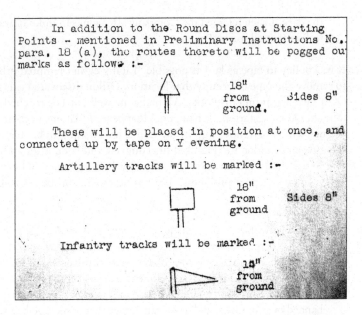

In addition to the Round Discs at Starting
Points - mentioned in Preliminary Instructions No.
para. 18 (a), the routes thereto will be pegged ou
marks as follows :-

⟨triangle flag symbol⟩   18"
                              from   Sides 8"
                              ground.

These will be placed in position at once, and
connected up by tape on Y evening.

Artillery tracks will be marked :-

⟨rectangular flag symbol⟩   18"
                              from   Sides 8"
                              ground

Infantry tracks will be marked :-

⟨pennant flag symbol⟩   18"
                              from
                              ground

X/Y Night: this phase began two nights before a Tank operation (X/Y night). In general it commenced principally with laying guidance tapes from their lying up place to the front line. Flags were also pegged out to guide the tanks. This was often undertaken by the RO's Orderly under the supervision of the RO. Experience showed that starting at the front line and working backward to the start point or, if it was necessary, as far back as the deployment or assembly points, was the most effective method. Tanks were expected to drive with the right track aligned to the two inch white tape with its quarter inch black stripe down the centre.[4] Each battlescape presented its own challenges. At the Third Ypres the ROs were working across a battlescape that had already been extensively shelled. Dillon remarked on the contrast between the Ypres and the Cambrai operations where

> ... as Company Reconnaissance Officer, it was my job to find the best route from our lying up place, some miles behind the lines, to the front. This was not so difficult as it was in the battle areas in which we had been engaged (Ypres). There had been little activity and, in view of the proposed absence of bombardment, there was not much in the way of artillery positions, dumps, trenches, &c (sic) to circumnavigate. I surveyed the route up to about 1200 yards from the front, when the area became congested ... This meant laying the white guiding tapes (with the black line in the centre) to enable us to dodge in and out of the various obstacles, e.g. trench junctions, or awkward pieces of ground, &c (sic) in

4   TNA, WO95/102, '2nd Brigade Tank Corps HQ 1 March 1918-31 October 1919'.

the dark. I then rejoined my Company after some 15 miles of walking, with the feeling that all was well.[5]

It was policy to tape as late as possible. Taping earlier tempted other units in the area to remove the tape or occupy that location. Dillon discovered this the following night (X/Y) when guiding his tanks. All had gone well until he reached the point where his tape should have started. 'It had gone! It appeared that one or more of the extra battery of guns which had moved up in the night, not wishing to be disturbed, had rolled up the tape and hidden it.'[6] He used his compass and later, after an hour's search, found the tape. It had been an agonising time for him and his relief can only be imagined. There could be other problems. The wrong tape could be used. Hammond cited an occasion when

> ... an elementary error, which could have had serious consequences occurred when tank routes were taped to the start line by reconnaissance officers and section commanders ... it was discovered that the tape drawn from tank brigade HQ was infantry not tank tape. But for the fact that the night was cloudless with a full moon, this mistake might have had the serious consequences. The tape was handed over in sacks, and as no tape other than tank tape had thus been issued for more than a year, it was not specially inspected to make sure it was all right.[7]

A greater hazard for ROs was taping under shell fire especially during the mobile warfare during the 'Hundred Days'. A Company RO, Lieutenant R.H. Ledger of 11th Tank Battalion, on 8 October 1918, led his tanks at night under very heavy shell-fire. He laid his tape right through the enemy outpost up to the German line whilst infantry action was actually taking place. 'He enabled the tanks to follow his tape and to get into position without the enemy being aware.'[8] Not unsurprisingly Ledger was awarded an MC for this action which took place near Villers-Outreaux, east of the St. Quentin canal.

The responsibility for taping routes was stressful. Dillon remarked that 'going up to the front, as I had to do many times to establish tank routes, or to familiarise tank officers with the way up and over was a strain.'[9] Browne, a former tank commander, confessed to 'the strain of conducting any approach march, however short and simple ... To go into action in a tank was, in a way, a lesser evil'.[10] Apparently Henriques

5   BLUL, Record of N.M. Dillon, p. 21.
6   Ibid., p. 21.
7   Hammond, 'The Theory and Practice of Tank Cooperation' (Unpublished thesis, University of Birmingham, 2005), p. 335.
8   Maurice, pp. 218-219, citation of the award of the M.C. to Lieut. R. H. Ledger.
9   BLUL, Record of N. M. Dillon, p.19 and Brown, D.G., *The Tank in Action*, p.484.
10   Browne, *The Tank in Action*, p. 485.

suffered similar 'strain and stress'.[11] Even the gallant Hotblack could be affected. 'He lost his nerve one time ... but it didn't affect his work ... we were walking through some very nasty shell fire rain storms and I knew perfectly well that his nerve had gone but it didn't make the slightest difference. He walked upright. No cowering down.'[12] However, not more than five ROs (6.75 percent) of the seventy-four listed in Appendix II have been identified as fatalities. They were Captain T.A. Nelson, Lieutenant R.A. Gatfield, Lieutenant J.L. Lees, Captain D.L. Monaghan and Lieutenant J. Black.[13] Dillon though was wounded three times during tank operations and Hotblack four times.

Y/Z Night: This was the time when the ROs guided the tanks from their place of assembly (tankodrome) to their start point. It is at this time that guidance tapes were checked since traffic may have broken or buried the tape or, as witnessed above, other armed units may have removed it. The Company RO in tandem with the unit commander (Company or Section) undertook a final briefing and ensured that the Tank Commanders had all the necessary materials to take them across no man's land. The RO then led the tanks along the tape to the start point behind the front to await Z hour.

This phase had its own hazards for the ROs. Dillon recounted a particularly heart stopping moment whilst guiding his company tanks before Cambrai:

On the Approach March I had one of those unpleasing experiences which are apt to occur when leading Tanks at night. I was walking ahead guiding, with a shrouded torch, when I got stuck in some barbed wire. I could not free myself and the leading Tank got closer. In desperation I shone my torch at full strength into the driver's visor, normally an unpardonable sin, and the Tank stopped to a profuse flow of language, half on top of me.[14]

On 26 November 1917 Second Lieutenant A.H.C. Borger of F Battalion 'guided twenty tanks to their assembly point unaided. Later, Lieutenant J.D. Kennedy of 8th Battalion, 'reconnoitred the best route for his company of tanks over the Hindenburg system going on ahead many times under machine gun fire' at Bellicourt.

On occasions, particularly if the three Sections of a Company had different start points, the Section Commander would guide his tanks. The first VC awarded to personnel in the Tank Corps was for reconnaissance and guiding a Section of tanks. Captain Clement Robertson, Section Commander, 1st Battalion, 1st Brigade,

11   Loewe, *Basil Henriques*, p. 48.
12   BLUL, Colonel Dillon Interview, Tape 520.
13   This figure has been obtained by cross-referencing names in the Tank Corps Roll of Honour with the names of those Killed in Action as they appear in Maurice, *Tank Corps Book of Honour.*
14   Dillon, Record of N. M. Dillon, p. 21.

reconnoitred the only bridge across the Reutelbeek on 4 October 1917. 'For three days and nights he and his servant, Private Allen (subsequently awarded the D.C.M.), went carefully backwards and forwards over the ground under heavy fire, taping the route for the Tanks.' The dark and misty weather made observation from the tanks even more difficult so Captain Robertson walked on ahead 'facing besides the shells an intense close-range machine-gun and rifle fire.' The tanks crossed the bridge and he led them further along the route. At this point Captain Robertson was shot through the head but 'the Tanks went on, and succeeded in their mission.'[15] This action was not unlike that of Hotblack in November 1916 on the Ancre for which he was awarded his first D.S.O.

On Y/Z night before the tank action at Messines Captain F. Vans Agnew, a former infantry officer, successfully guided his Section without the assistance of an RO. His colonel detailed him to guide his Section of tanks into action and dispense with the need for tapes. This was because he had spent five months in these very trenches in 1915 and, as they were very little altered, he apparently knew them perfectly well.[16] By contrast was the abortive attack near Proyart on 10 August 1918 by 7 Section, 2 Company, 8th (H) Tank Battalion. It was led by the Section Commander, Captain D.E. Hickey, in support of the Australians. All the ingredients of failure were there: no Tank Corps RO but an infantry scout instead; no prior reconnaissance; a daylight approach march followed by a night attack.[17]

Z Day. The Battalion and Company ROs were tasked to observe the start of the battle before following up the attack behind the second wave of tanks and infantry. At the opening of the Cambrai offensive Henriques recalled that his 'job was to watch the advance and then report ... at 7 o'clock I moved forward with the infantry'.[18] It was during this phase that the majority of Military Crosses (MCs) were awarded to ROs. In total 47 percent of the ROs listed earlier were decorated.[19] Henriques was Mentioned in Dispatches (gazetted January 1918).

Whilst the Battalion RO reported to his commander the Company RO reconnoitred 'the ground *en route* with a view to finding the best approach for supply and reserve Tanks ... and study the ground ahead'. They reported any mistakes made. Close communication between the two ROs took place to exchange information required by Senior or Tank Commanders. It was often necessary for both ROs to 'prepare fresh Tank routes for a possible resumption of the attack ... if the final objective has not been reached'. At Messines Captain R.C. Knight of B Battalion 'reconnoitred routes through the enemy system after its capture and led Army Reserve over them. He also

15 Williams-Ellises, *The Tank Corps*, pp. 96-97. See also Maurice, p. 71.
16 J. Vans, J. & P. Widdowson, *Veteran Volunteer* (Barnsley, Pen & Sword, 2014), p. 60.
17 Hickey, *Rolling into Action*, pp. 237-244.
18 Loewe, *Basil Henriques: A Portrait*, p. 49.
19 Maurice, *Tank Corps Book of Honour*, pp. 85-234.

proceeded on foot to the Oostaverne Line and collected valuable information with a view to future operations'.[20] During the same battle Second Lieutenant J.M. Bailey of A Battalion 'followed up the tanks during their advance on Wytschaete and brought back most valuable information as to their position and condition.'[21] Later he added a Croix de Guerre to his MC. Temporary Captain D.T. Raikes added a bar to his MC when at Villers-Bretonneux on 8 August 1918 he 'closely followed his company on foot, horseback and bicycle, as he found the means, re-directing his tanks as the situation demanded.'[22] The *Tank Corps Book of Honour* also recorded a number of occasions that ROs exceeded their duties during a battle.

Between 8 and 11 August, during the Battle of Amiens, an RO, Lieutenant James Lowry Lees of the 6th (F) Tank battalion, 'took command of a tank, capturing two machine guns' and later 'crawled out to a derelict tank … and though heavily shelled he manned the gun and silenced enemy snipers.'[23] Lieutenant N.M. Dillon at Arras, although only a trainee RO at the time, took command of a tank after the commander was killed.[24] Major F.E. Hotblack's adventures during the Cambrai[25] and the Hindenburg Line[26] offensives became Tank Corps legends. Although the ROs followed up their tanks usually behind the second wave, they were not safe from injury. During both the Cambrai and Amiens operations Dillon added to the wound he received in the Lens area (see above). During Cambrai 'I was following the Tanks with the infantry when a bullet split my thumb and cast my walking stick (now displayed in the Tank Corps Museum) some 50 yards behind me. There was very little firing, and I think there must have been a German overrun and hiding, who had a shot at me.'[27] He resisted evacuation to England fearing he might not return to B (2nd) Battalion. He had faced a greater hazard during the Third Ypres.

When following up his tanks Dillon and his orderly took refuge in a tunnel under the Menin Road since 'all hell was coming down.' It was also a Brigadier's HQ. Whilst seeking shelter a Major entered and requested the assistance of the tanks after his infantry were held up at 'Jap Trench'.

> So there was nothing for it but to "do and dare". I was not religiously inclined, but I remember asking for courage to help me. I got it and set forth. There was the usual featureless terrain and the usual shelled ground. Owing to the slight elevation, it was not bogged and I made comparatively good speed, and reach John Riordan's Tank. To talk to a Tank in action was not easy, there were too

20   Ibid., p. 91
21   Ibid., p.91
22   Ibid., p. 156.
23   Ibid., p. 148.
24   BLUL, Record of M.D.Dillon, p. 18.
25   Cooper, *The Ironclads of Cambrai*, p. 161.
26   Williams-Ellises, *The Tank Corps*, pp. 253-254.
27   BLUL, Record of M. D. Dillon, pp. 21-22.

many Germans equally anxious to do so, but with other motives. Eventually I got round to the front and, partly sheltered by the horns of the Tank, I rattled on the driver's visor. John R. looked out with great surprise at seeing me, and I told him what the Brigadier had said about the infantry not being able to advance on Jap Trench. I saw him well away and disappear into the cloud of smoke normal to these proceedings.[28]

On the opening day of the Amiens offensive, 8 August 1918, Dillon was again wounded and although initially thought not to be serious complications occurred later. According to his own account and the unit war diary, he, together with his Battalion commander, Lieutenant Colonel E.D. Bryce, the Regimental Sergeant-Major and three Orderlies, followed the tanks along the main road to Warfusée-Aubercourt. 'On reaching the outskirts of WARFUSEE-ABERCOURT (sic) hostile shelling became rather severe, and Captain DILLON was wounded in both legs while crossing the road with me. While his wounds were being attended to by my Medical Orderly 6 German Officers came out of a dug-out and surrendered.'[29] Many years later Dillon recalled the event slightly differently. He reported that he 'got a piece of aluminium nose cap in the left ankle, which lodged between the Achilles (sic) tendon and the bone. It was painful because it burnt, being the fuse of the shell. I also received sundry small wounds, mainly in the back. I could not walk, and so this was the end of the war for me.'[30] He was carried to the field Dressing Station by a number of German prisoners before being taken by ambulance and train to Amiens then on to Boulogne and the hospital ship *Pieter der König* thence to a 'privately supplied hospital in a house in Mayfair.'

Post Battle Duties. At the conclusion of the battle there were reports to write and submit.[31] There was particular concern about the limited literary skills of Tank Commanders. The recommendation was that the knowledgeable and talented RO should 'help Tank Commanders in writing their Battle History sheets which are notoriously badly written at present.' It endorsed the idea that the 'clear minded' RO should cross-examine the Tank Commander and they submit a joint report.[32] The Battalion and Company ROs submitted their own after action reports which included recommendations for future operations. To take one example from the Messines operation which also provides an illustration of the ROs' after action reports: Captain R.C. Knight the RO of B (2nd) Battalion reported:

28   Dillon, Record if D.M. Dillon, p. 19.
29   TNA, 2nd (B) Battalion War Diary. TNA nomenclature needed M.
30   BLUL, Record of D. M. Dillon, p.26.
31   TNA, WO95/118, *6th Brigade Training Centre, 1 January 1917–30 November 1919.*
32   TNA, WO95/104, *War Experiences, Reconnaissance and Intelligence Duties*, p. 10.

1. **Preliminary** (Work) indicating that the ROs visited the area two months before the attack confining their reconnaissance to the back areas and the British trenches. He complained, although it was not clear about whom, that 'the work was considerably handicapped by the fact that Half Way Halting Places and Points of Deployment had already been chosen' and that 'secrecy can be carried too far, and Reconnaissance Officers must be allowed to use their discretion. There was good use of the plentiful Observation Posts (OPs).

2. **Maps and Photographs**: The Battalion received 890 maps (225 maps for each Company) of which the 1/5000 maps were the most valuable for Tank Commanders. He opined that 'one good oblique photo showing a Tank Commander's route is worth 1000 vertical photos to him ... the Battalion received 1649 photos and Companies 425, 403 and 574 respectively.

3. **Plasticine Model**; it appeared that only 6 Company valued these (see below).

4. **Trained Draughtsmen** were essential and each Battalion should have at least one or two.

5. **Obstacles**: Knight was principally concerned with marshy ground created by the heavy shelling along the Steenbeek.

6. **Tank Defences**: here the concern was for craters, anti-tank guns and armour piercing ammunition.

7. **Work Done on Y.Z. and A. Days**:[33] here he referred to the reports of the Company ROs. On Y day landmarks should be inspected and shown to the Tank Commanders while on Z day the Battalion RO is most use at Battalion HQ until 'at least Z plus 2 (hours)'. A day was spent preparing for a further attack.

8. **Miscellaneous**: under this heading Knight included
    • The need for ROs to go over no man's land in a tank.
    • The need of motor cycles for communications.
    • The efficient work of the Brigade I.O. in getting maps and photos out.
    • The necessity of ensuring that the ROs brief the Tank Commanders by making it a 'parade', that is, an order.
    • The need to supply the ROs with telescopes, periscopes and drawing implements.

33 'A Day' is the day after an attack.

- The need to have up to date information by daily visits to Corps and Division Intelligence offices.[34]

The R.O. of No. 6 Company, B Battalion was Second Lieutenant J.C. Jinks. His appended report provided one of the bases for Captain Knight's report. He fully concurred with his senior officer regarding maps, photographs, Draughtsmen, the need for a motor cycle, the problem posed by the Steenbeek and enemy anti-tank defences adding that the armour piercing bullets did not penetrate the thicker plating of the Mark IV Tank. He also made a point of reporting that a plasticine model 'of the area was made and the more important features e.g. farms, woods etc. labelled. Later, when the tank routes were settled, each route was marked on the model so that each tank commander could see the ground over which he was likely to travel.' More specifically:

> On Y day, I called on both the 25th and 36th Divisions for the latest information and also went to the O. P. on MONT KEMMEL. New photographs were explained to the Tank Commanders. These were only of use in showing the condition of the ground, as nearly all landmarks had been obliterated. On Y. Z. night, I saw that each tank Commander had his maps and photographs properly placed in his tank and went up with one pair to the Starting Point.
>
> On Z. mornign [sic] I was with the O. C. Coy. at Zero and saw the Corps Reserve Section on the proper way. I then went up as far as the STEENEBECK, and guided the Corps Reserve Section for a short time. I then returned and reported to the O. C. Coy. remaining with him for the rest of the day and visiting all the tanks of the Company.
>
> On 'A' day I got in touch immediately with the R. O. 'B' Battalion for information and orders. The 2 divisions were also visited later. I went forward to the line of posts on reconnaissance duties.

Reconnaissance during the 'Hundred Days': it has already been suggested that the post-Amiens campaign of mobile warfare imposed different challenges for the ROs. The reduced number of tanks meant there was for the most part a return to 'penny packet' operations. The exceptions were the attacks on the Drocourt-Quéant and the Hindenburg Lines (1and 29 September respectively) and the crossing of the Rivers Selle and Sambre (17-20 October). ROs still generally employed the activities and skills they used in the set piece attacks. The increased tempo of operations meant that the time available for reconnaissance was limited and consequently 'very hurried'.[35]

---

34   TNA, WO95/101, '2nd Tank Brigade HQ February-December 1917'.
35   TNA, WO95/108, 4th Tank Brigade Report on Operations, August 22nd to24th, 1918, 28August 1918 and Hammond, *The Theory and Practice of Tank Cooperation with Other Arms During the First World War*, p. 336.

ROs often undertook reconnaissance over old and known ground. Command and control had also become much looser.[36] Around 20 August and before he was posted back to England Henriques provided the reconnaissance for his battalion of tanks that captured Ablainzeville, Achiet le Petit, Sapigny and Beugny all in an arc north of Bapaume.[37]

The declining number of tanks was now spread across three armies: the Fourth, Third and the Canadian Corps of the First. The geographical challenge for the ROs was to get their tanks across three successive but contrasting 'battlescapes'. The 1st, 2nd and 3rd Tank Brigades were initially guided across a landscape that 'was divided with curious exactness into two kinds' that affected tank operations.[38] North of Puisieux the battlescape 'bore some resemblance to a state of nature.' But 'southwards to the Somme was one vast nondescript expanse of ruin, broken only by a few stumps or a cloud of dust' of the old and again recently fought over Somme battlefield.[39] The only advantage was that the main rivers (Somme, Ancre, Sensée, and Scarpe) offered few obstacles as the tanks advanced parallel to them unlike the canals. The second area to the east, beyond Bapaume, 'the whole of this country was bare rolling grassland … dotted with a large number of hutted camps … and trees around the various villages … the roads were sunken in places, and there was a general resemblance to parts of Salisbury Plain, except the undulations were less pronounced.'[40] This was the area previously occupied by the BEF following the German withdrawal in February-March of 1917. Here the ROs possessed maps and knowledge of the area but were faced with the major obstacles of the Canal de Nord and St. Quentin Canal. Captain D. G. Browne was awarded his M.C. for his part in the successful reconnaissance of the former (see earlier). Beyond the Hindenburg Line the ROs were faced with unknown territory for which they had few maps. This was a pristine battlescape.[41] Villages were intact and their churches still offered observation posts. Undestroyed woods provided cover for anti-tank guns. It has already be noted that beyond Le Cateau the land took on an appearance closer to the Normandy bocage with its smaller fields bound by hedges and fences.[42]

Reconnaissance work under the conditions of the 'continuous battle' demanded a different perspective ('terrain evaluation') of the battlescape. Now 'a general and wide

36   J. Boff, *Winning and Losing on the Western Front* (Cambridge, University Press, 2012), pp. 140-145.
37   Army Personnel Centre, Glasgow,(*Army Form B.199, Henriques' Military Service Papers*).
38   Peter Simkins, 'Somme Reprise: Reflections on the Fighting for Albert and Bapaume, August 1918' in Brian Bond, et al, *Look to Your Front: Studies in the First World War by the British Commission of Military History* (Staplehurst, Spellmount,1999), p. 156.
39   Browne, *The Tank in Action'*, p. 383.
40   Ibid., p. 419.
41   WO 95/100, '12th Tank Battalion War History', p.35.
42   It is instructive to undertake a computer transect from Albert to Mons using 'Google Earth' in order to appreciate some of these distinctions.

view' rather than 'a particular view of one sector' was necessary.' This was especially so because the Germans were perfecting a fighting retreat with 'defence in depth' tactics. Since the 'time for reconnaissance preparations will be almost always inadequate ... there must be no risk of Tanks suddenly called upon in the evening of one day to fight at dawn the next day, failing to reach their starting points because of inadequate reconnaissance.'[43] Hence the ROs were instructed to take every opportunity when there was a break in the battle to reconnoitre as far ahead as possible. Fortunately the new battlescape 'East of the (Albert-Arras) railway was full of well-marked features' and the tanks were 'in little danger of getting lost'.[44]

The demands of mobile warfare required a reassessment of some basic techniques. 'It is realized that the rapidity with which operations must now necessarily be planned and put into execution makes the employment of many aids to reconnaissance impossible, but every effort must be made to adapt the reconnaissance to the situation'.[45] RO mapping changed from linear route presentation to determining the area of individual tank operation. The front line could move quickly forward before air photographs reached the ROs and be properly studied. At the same time the battlescape offered greater opportunities for German anti-tank defences. In spite of *Panzerschrechen*[46] villages, orchards and woodland concealed the tank's deadliest enemy – the anti-tank gun. German mines, tank traps and anti-tank rifles were less effective.[47] ROs with the assistance of No. 8 Squadron RAF, commanded by Major Trafford Leigh-Mallory (later of Battle of Britain fame in the Second World War), worked with limited success to determine the location of enemy anti-tank artillery and destroy it.[48]

It is perhaps no coincidence that it was during this post-Amiens phase of mobile warfare that concern was shown that the ROs were exercising too great a degree of independence.[49] This was a time when circumstances warranted the devolution of decision making across the whole BEF including the Tank Corps. It was a view expressed as far back as the 7 June 1917 when 2nd Tank Brigade suggested that 'decentralisation is absolutely necessary'.[50] ROs were now spread amongst fewer and fewer tanks

---

43   TNA, WO95/102, 'Report on Operations, 21 August-3 September 1918', 7 September 1918.

44   Ibid.

45   Ibid., In earlier positional warfare the ROs' ashplant stick was used to test the weight-bearing nature of the ground. In undertaking reconnaissance over a former battlefield during mobile operations the ash stick was more useful for detecting old barbed wire and holes in deep grass. See Browne, *The Tank in Action*, p. 442.

46   A term used by German First Quarter Master-General Erich von Ludendorff meaning 'fear of tanks'.

47   It has already been noted that the one lethal minefield that destroyed 5 of 12 tanks of the American 301 Tank Company was seeded by the British Fifth Army.

48   Boff, *Winning and Losing on the Western Front*, pp. 175-176.

49   TNA, *WO95/104,(War Experiences)*, p. 9.

50   TNA, WO95/101, '2nd Army Operations, 7th June 1917, Report on Reconnaissance Work by 2nd Brigade, H.B., M.G.C.', Appendix A, p. 5.

An Armoured car. (TCMA)

so that a Company RO had to guide into action only one or two tanks from a unit that had been formed into a composite company. At the same time the demands for support from the infantry increased precipitately. This was the situation that Browne experienced with the Canadians at both Beugny (30 August 1918) on the Bapaume-Cambrai road, and Sancourt (30 September 1918), north of Cambrai.[51] In the former instance:

> ... having found Beale, the Reconnaissance Officer of B Company, with his tanks, I walked forward with him past Favreuil to some rising ground near Beugnâtre. We wished to see something of the countryside before us while the light held ... we sat for some time in a trench, memorising as much as we could verify on the map. Camps of Nissen huts were clustered about Beugnâtre, and others seemed to extend far over the monotonous plain behind towards Beugny. It was agreed between us that our sections should move together by the track we had just followed to within a few hundred yards of Beugnâtre, when Beale would lead his tanks south of the village while I took mine round by the north.

51   Browne, *The Tank in Action*, pp. 419-427 and 482-493.

The local action at Sancourt was a relatively small affair involving just three tanks, but it was a minor disaster since there were twenty-one casualties out of a total of twenty-four tank crew members. Browne claimed that it was caused by mismanagement on the part of 12th Canadian Brigade, an 'accumulation of blunders ... quite exceptional in the Canadian Corps' which left the C. O. and RO of 7 (H) Tank Brigade without orders, a changed zero hour of which they were not informed, liaison with a Canadian Intelligence Officer who did not know that the tanks were cooperating in the action and inaccurate information concerning the German occupation of the village. 'So ended, as far as the 7th Tank Battalion was concerned, not only this miserable and inexcusable fiasco at Sancourt, but all direct participation in the war.'[52]

The end of this period of mobile warfare may also have anticipated the eventual replacement of the specialist Tank Reconnaissance Officer. It witnessed what Brigadier General David Henderson described as 'contact reconnaissance' (Chapter 3). In the last few days of the war the mobile 17th (Armoured Car) Battalion of 3rd Tank Brigade was in support of the advancing Fourth Army. The Tank Brigade reported that 'the cars were chiefly used for reconnaissance and engaging machine guns'.[53]

---

52   Browne, *The Tank in Action*, p. 493.
53   TNA, WO95/105, *3rd Brigade HQ January 1918 to 1919*. This may be an instance when 'contact reconnaissance' was undertaken: See Henderson, *The Art of Reconnaissance*, p. 11.

13

Protective Reconnaissance

The 'Protective Reconnaissance' in which the ROs engaged included two phases. They might be described as the 'Defensive Phase' and the 'Reactive Phase'. In the Defensive Phase between December 1917 and 21 March 1918 the activities and skills employed by the ROs were still broadly similar to those discussed in both the Offensive and Training Phases. It was the operational context that was essentially different. Until December 1917 the Tank Corps had been employed in an offensive capacity in positional warfare. The tanks were valued for their 'break in' and 'break through' tactics. The work of the ROs was structured accordingly. Now they were on the 'back foot' and protective reconnaissance was the principal activity as a major German offensive was anticipated following the Russian surrender. Between 21 March 1918 and the end of June 1918 the Reconnaissance Branch were reacting to the German Spring Offensive. The initial German thrust, 'Operation Michael', against the British Third and Fifth Armies south of Arras, was the overture to the 'Kaiserschlacht' (the Emperor's Battle). It was followed by 'Operation Georgette', known to the British as the 'Lys Offensive', between Ypres and La Bassée (9 – 28 April). In the first week of 'Michael' the ROs were supporting the tanks in their defensive response to the enemy advance. Later the ROs found themselves fighting as infantrymen.

Defensive Phase. In the report of 16 Infantry Brigade following Cambrai the question of using tanks in a defensive capacity was raised. This might be the origin of the defensive tactic later known to the Tank Corps as the 'Savage Rabbit' policy:

> It was felt that if one or two of the tanks had been hidden in the vicinity and had come out as hostile infantry advanced, they could have rendered invaluable assistance. It is suggested that the use of tanks, camouflaged or concealed, ready to assist counter attacks should be considered. They should have an active defensive role as well as purely offensive.[1]

---

1   LHMA, I/3/be,18. *Suggested Use of Tanks in Defence*, p. 5.

At this point the Tank Corps had no clear policy of their role in defence. In response to the German counter attacks on 30 November tanks operated in driblets unsupported by the infantry. Hence they suffered heavy losses. What was clear was that from mid-January 1918 the Tank Corps waited in anticipation or a German offensive.

> The story of the Tank Corps from the beginning of February to nearly the end of March 1918 is one of waiting and expectancy, of strategic moves to unexpected places, of diligent rehearsal for first nights upon which the curtain never arose, of endless preparations for events that never happened.[2]

The 370 tanks 'fit for action' (320 Mark IVs and 50 'Whippets) in thirteen Battalions were formed into 'a defensive cordon stretching from about Roisel northwards to a little south of Bethune-a frontage of some sixty miles'.[3]

Lieutenant-Colonel E. B. Hankey with the Fifth Army ordered his 4thTank Brigade ROs on 10 February to prepare for this eventuality by undertaking 'reconnaissance in the area where tanks maybe required to function'. He added that it was 'a large one' since the tanks were thin on the ground. He recognized that 'time is an important factor' therefore they should 'concentrate on our front from where the enemy is most likely to be expected'. They were also ordered to reconnoitre 'back areas which the tanks may have to pass over'.[4] The action they were expected to undertake was in accordance with SS203, *Instructions for Anti-Tank Defence (Provisional), February 1918*, p. 9. Hotblack may well have had a leading part to play in the preparation of this document. Beach wrote that 'as the Tank Corps' lead intelligence officer … Hotblack became the BEF's de facto expert on German Tanks'.[5] However, in the event, the German Order of Battle only included 9 tanks.[6] Reconnaissance Officers became closely involved since they were required to have 'an intimate knowledge of the ground and defences' and that 'routes and areas of manoeuvre must be carefully thought out and arranged beforehand'. They thoroughly reconnoitred 1,500 square miles of country and also established the location of supply dumps.[7] They then had to instruct the Tank Commanders regarding the 'knowledge of the ground and defences

2   Williams-Ellises, *The Tank Corps*, p. 153.
3   Fuller, *Tanks in the Great War 1914-18*, pp. 172-173. Browne, *The Tank in Action*, p. 352 claims there were 270 tanks. It is more than likely that Fuller's figure is the correct one.
4   WO95/108, '4th Brigade HQ, December 1918-March 1919', orders of Lieutenant Colonel Edward Barnard Hankey. He was promoted to Brigadier-General in April 1918.
5   James Beach, 'British Intelligence and German tanks, 1916-18', *War in History*, Vol. 144, pp. 454-475 and Scouting for Brigands, pp. 124-133.
6   Zabecki, D. T., 'The German 1918 Offensive', *Strategy and History*, (Abingdon, Routledge, 2006.), p. 137-138 and Ralf Raths, From the *Bremerwagen* to the A7V: German Tank Production and Armoured Warfare, 1916-1918, in Searle, *Genesis, Employment, Aftermath*, pp. 95-102.
7   Fuller, *Tanks in the Great War 1914-18*, p.173.

in the Sector where they will operate'.[8] Browne in his new role as an RO with A Company, 7th Battalion, 1st Tank Brigade was located in the coalfield area of Artois (Gohelle) where day after day he

> Tramped about the melancholy region behind our lines, exploring roads, examining bridges, selecting lying-up points, repeating every journey half a dozen times with our parties of learners, like a pair of Cook's couriers. 'On your left you now see Fosse 16, *dit de Lens*; beyond is Fosse 7, *de Bethune*. That handsome edifice far in front – it is not advisable to try and reach it – is the Metallurgique factory at Wingles.' I have never been so heartily wearied of any piece of country as I became of the Lens coalfield.[9]

As it happened this was the one region the German Spring Offensive ignored.

The ROs had the particular responsibility for selecting places within the 'battle zone' from which individual tanks, camouflaged or hidden, could support the infantry and ambush the enemy instead of holding them further back in readiness for a counter attack.[10] This policy of static defence was not well received by Fuller at Tank Corps HQ. It was Elles who dubbed it a 'savage rabbit' policy. At the same time the Tank Corps intended to complete its winter training which included tuition in reconnaissance work. (See Chapter 9)

Reactive Phase. The rapid advance of the German army on the 21 March and subsequent days rendered most of the preparations ineffective.[11] The tanks did participate in a number of counter-attacks.[12] Along the Cambrai-Bapaume road, Captain Eric Quillaume, RO of the 8th Tank Battalion, on 21 March, 'showed conspicuous bravery in going forward under heavy machine-gun and shell fire, to reconnoitre and the successful counter-attack on Doignes was greatly due to his work. Three days later he repeated his 'excellent reconnaissance work under heavy artillery fire' to enable further counter-attacks on nearby Barastre, Bus and Haplincourt.[13] He was awarded a Military Cross. Lieutenant E. Whiteside, a former Territorial Force officer, now a Company RO in 10th Tank Battalion, led his company in a successful night counter attack near Gommecourt when he 'personally guided the tanks into action and, although subject to heavy shell and machine-gun fire, he continued to lead the tanks

---

8   TNA, WO 95/108 (no date).
9   Browne, *The Tank in Action*, p. 325.
10   Dillon is also critical of the defensive policy in a subsequent interview with Peter Liddle (BLUL).
11   Only 48.5% of tanks were in action. Fuller, *Tanks in the Great War, 1916-18*, p. 177.
12   Hammond, 'The Theory and Practice of Tank Cooperation with Other Arms on the Western Front During the First World War', pp. 245-252.
13   Maurice, *Tank Corps Roll of Honour*, p.124.

Abandoned Tanks near Brie-sur-Somme. (TCMA)

and enabled them to engage the enemy successfully causing heavy casualties to be inflicted.' He also was awarded an MC.[14]

The task of the ROs in the great retreat was more often to guide the tanks to safety. Their success was limited as the slow-moving tanks were by-passed, outflanked and encircled.[15] Many tank supply dumps were captured.[16] At least the ROs' mobility and knowledge of both the ground and the tanks was an asset. Captain Elton was awarded his MC for his gallantry in tank counter-attacks, information gathering, communicating with isolated tanks and 'fighting on foot with Lewis guns.'[17] The ROs played an important role in the communications between tanks and unit commanders.[18] They rallied the tanks and guided them to crossing points of the Somme. They were not always successful as tanks ran out of petrol and bridges were demolished before they arrived there. Seventeen tanks of the 5th Tank Battalion attempted to cross the Somme at Brie, south of Peronne. Unfortunately the bridge had been destroyed so the tanks were abandoned and wrecked after their Lewis guns had been salvaged.[19]

The ROs now found themselves operating without their tanks. They joined their fellow 'unhorsed' Tank Officers as infantrymen. 'The Tank-less crews were formed

14   Ibid,, *The Tank Corps*, p. 131.
15   Williams-Ellises, *The Tank Corps, p*, 161.
16   A temporary success was achieved at Beugny, Fuller, *Tanks in the Great War 1914-18*, p. 174.
17   Maurice, *Tank Corps Roll of Honour*, p. 122.
18   Mitchell, *Tank Warfare*, p. 179.
19   Williams-Ellises, *The Tank Corps*, p. 163.

into Lewis gun detachments'.[20] In this role they performed bravely. Second Lieutenant B. S. Carter, for example, a RO with 5th Tank Battalion, was awarded the MC for gallantry near Meteren on April 16 1918:

> This officer was reconnaissance officer of his company ... when the enemy broke through ... and our infantry began to withdraw in small parties. Lieut. Carter left his position and came out into the open, rallied and reorganised these parties, and took up a line where the enemy was eventually checked. All this was done under close range machine-gun fire. 2nd Lieut. Carter held the line until relieved.[21]

In a letter to his wife Captain B.L.Q. Henriques described in some detail his actions along the Lys Canal where General Elles was present to rally the infantry. He describes how he had been ordered to support the infantry with a detachment of machine guns under the command of a Major Norton. When they were attacked in the rear Henriques reported the situation to the infantry Divisional HQ.

> After I had been there an hour a runner came back to say that Norton had been wounded, and soon after we heard that the enemy had broken through North (sic) of the Canal. Just at that moment General Elles (G.O.C. Tanks) came up and asked what the situation was and having heard it ... said he would go up and see for himself. He had his A.D.C. with him and took me along as well ... he went out beyond the withdrawing infantry and chose an exposed spot, sat down amid a torrent of machine gun bullets, took out his map and had a council of war. He then sent me back a couple of hundred yards and told me to stop every man on a certain cross-roads, reorganise them and make them take up fresh positions. This I did and thus we re-established the line.

Henriques was decorated with the Italian Silver Star and was again 'Mentioned in Dispatches' (gazetted in June 1918) for his work here.[22]

As has been described above the ROs of 1st Tank Brigade were removed from these events. They were in support of I Corps in the Bethune-Lens area. Their task was more frustrating than dangerous. Between April and June they were involved in preparing for counter-attacks, 'the celebrated "Delta" Scheme ... whose ramifications were to keep the Reconnaissance Officers of all three Battalions busy for the next month ... for there was a great shortage of accurate maps.'[23] The scheme was never

20 Ibid., p. 168.
21 Maurice, *Tank Corps Roll of Honour*, p. 133.
22 Loewe, *Basil Henriques*, p. 52. Williams-Ellises in *The Tank Corps*, pp. 168-169 quotes at greater length from this letter, ascribing it to 'a Reconnaissance Officer'.
23 WO 95/100, '12th Tank Battalion, History, chapter 3', pp. 10-12. Initially it was aimed to relieve Bethune if necessary but was aborted at least twice and 'died hard... with the

launched. After Amiens the depleted Tank Corps would return to the offensive but in the context of mobile operations.

As the First World War drew to a close so did the role of the specialist Tank Intelligence and Reconnaissance Officers. After recovering from the wound he received at Amiens Captain N. M. Dillon MC was posted back to Bovington in November 1918 where he had 'nothing to do' except instruct 'one class of six' in reconnaissance work. Then 'the Reconnaissance School was closed up, its need having gone'.[24]

German retreat from the Lys salient.'
24 BLUL, M. N. Dillon Report, p. 27.

14

Conclusions

This study of Tank Corps' Intelligence and Reconnaissance work has endeavoured to describe and analyse a neglected but important aspect of British tank operations in the Great War on the Western Front between1916-18 and thereby fill a gap in the early historiography of the Tank Corps. It is an attempt to provide a more comprehensive account than has yet been given of the Tank Corps' Reconnaissance Department. It encompasses the wide variety of activities undertaken by the Corps' Intelligence and Reconnaissance Officers in the First World War. In the first instance an outline of the historiography of tank operations was given to show and explain why virtually no attention has been paid to this important unit of the Tank Corps. The offensive and defensive operational efficiency of the tanks depended in the first instance on the work of these officers. It was thought helpful to place Tank Corps' reconnaissance work in its historical context especially during the decade before the Great War. The first tank operations in September 1916 had only this experience to depend upon at their baptism. However, past experience proved to have serious limitations when applied to this new technical arm. It accordingly was expedient to establish within the emerging Tank Corps a specialist Intelligence and Reconnaissance Department. Whilst the works of Hammond and Beach have been helpful in understanding the activities of these specialists, it still required a conceptual framework to be established in which the analysis of the Tank Corps' reconnaissance activities could take place. There was also a need to clarify the terminology employed. It was felt helpful to consider and employ the ideas of the original Intelligence and Reconnaissance Officers, especially Clough Williams-Ellis, to appreciate their activities. As a result the concept of 'Reconography' was borrowed to embrace their duties. At the same time the experiences of a number of these Intelligence and Reconnaissance Officers have been used to both illustrate and hopefully enliven the accounts of reconnaissance activities. This approach has, it is believed, given a valid picture of the activities of the Tank Corps Reconnaissance Branch. Between1916 and 1918 the work of the Reconnaissance Officers was determined by four considerations (the 4Ts): Technology (in this instance the tank), Tactics (the employment of the tanks), Terrain (the battlescape) and Training (of the Tank Commanders). Their work included first and second hand observations, collation and analysis of information together with its representation in graphical form before communicating and employing it in practice. Hence the use of the umbrella term 'Reconography'. The IOs and ROs also had an important role in the instruction of other tank officers in reconnaissance work which ultimately together with improved technology and tactics would make the ROs themselves redundant.

Hammond has shown how Field Service Regulations 1 (Operations), ergonomic limitations and infantry tactics influenced Tank Corps operations.[1] This also affected reconnaissance activities. The first tank commanders failed to apply *FSR Part I*. This was partly due to the urgent requirement for tanks for the Flers-Courcelette operation together with the imperative to learn other tank handling skills. At first there was also a mind-set on the part of GHQ that the tanks would operate only as important adjuncts to the infantry. The mechanical limitations of this new weapon were not fully understood by the infantry. It is to the credit of GHQ that these problems were eventually recognized and they supported the establishment of a Reconnaissance Department under Captain, later Major, F. E. Hotblack within the new Tank Corps HQ at Bermicourt. His leadership qualities set high standards for his Department.

As might have been anticipated with any innovation, the new Department experienced a number of tensions within the Corps. It reflected well on the open-mindedness of the Corps that these difficulties never detracted from what became one of the most efficient units in the BEF. The suggestion made that ROs might tend to become a state within a state (an *Imperium in Imperio*) has not so far been generally confirmed by all Tank Brigade commanders in War Diaries, 'After Action Reports' or Brigade histories. However, there is a considerable amount of evidence to suggest that the ROs did form an elite caste within the Tank Corps. Their superior reconnaissance and graphical talents, their intellect, communication and graphical skills and teaching abilities set them apart from the Tank Commanders. They were the 'Professors' of the Corps with a touch of eccentricity about them especially when they worked covertly. The ROs were mobile, independent and had privileged access to information. They rubbed shoulders and dined with the most senior commanders. They formed a small coterie of officers that messed and worked closely together behind the frontline in more salubrious circumstances than their Tank Officer brothers in arms. Most of their work took place safely behind the lines or in secret when they moved up to the front. During an attack (combat reconnaissance) they operated behind the leading tanks but experienced relatively few casualties. They came to exercise operational control over tank commanders for route selection and camouflage.

The original intention of *Standing Orders* in 1917 was that ROs would merely reconnoitre and advise on tank routes. Unit and tank commanders would take the decisions. In practice this division of responsibilities did not work. Fortunately, as befits a new and innovative arm that encouraged 'thinking outside the box' and characteristic of

---

1   Hammond, 'The Theory and Practice of Tank Cooperation with other Arms on the Western Front during the First World War'.

the BEF generally, 'the situation favoured experience over theory, the pragmatic over the programmatic'.[2] The responsibilities of the ROs increased accordingly giving them a decisive role in determining tank routes instead of Tank Commanders and a Staff (Tactical) support role with their Unit Commanders. All these activities enhanced their elite position. Attention was drawn to a further concern of unit commanders as to the relative importance of primary reconnaissance (field work) and secondary reconnaissance (office work).

The evidence indicates that generally the ROs were eminently successful in their primary role of getting their tanks to the start line, particularly for set piece offences in spite of the fog and friction of war. The failures that occurred were more often due to mechanical problems, weather conditions or poor driving. They had to meet the sometimes unrealistic expectations of infantry commanders. The ROs were equally successful in the continuous training of Tank Commanders with the expressed aim of making them skilled and their own reconnaissance experts. The critical role of the Reconnaissance Officer continued for only a short time after the Armistice. In the last few weeks of the war when tanks were fewer and operations increasingly mobile the role of the armoured car as a reconnaissance vehicle was increasingly employed. The need for a specialist Intelligence and Reconnaissance Department was at an end although the 'reconnaissance imperative'[3] would continue. In the First World War Tank Corps Reconnaissance Officers were successfully employed for just a brief two years in the service of a little understood, experimental and almost blind weapon for which they provided the eyes. Their legacy, however, was considerable. The German Panzer General, Heinz Guderian, based his blueprint for Panzer operations in the Second World War on his analysis principally of British tank operations in the Great War albeit relying on the controversial works of J.F.C. Fuller and Basil Liddell Hart.[4] He gives primary importance to the role of tank reconnaissance now employing more mobile methods. Readers will now be familiar with the concepts.

> The assault is preceded by **reconnaissance** covering the approach routes and assembly areas, the likely ground for the attack is provided by the study of maps, evaluation of aerial photographs, interrogation of prisoners and other sources of intelligence ... the **approach marches** are accomplished under cover of darkness, the flow of supplies is concealed, and the movement of traffic at night is kept under close control. We assume that the tank force are brought up to their assembly areas by night and without lights, using routes that have been identified beforehand, and which are well signposted and have been kept clear for them. As a general rule the assembly areas should be out of range of the enemy artillery, so

2   Boff, *Winning and Losing on the Western Front*, p. 249.
3   Beach, 'Scouting for Brigands', in Searle (ed), *Genesis, Employment, Aftermath*, p. 109.
4   Heinz Guderian, *Achtung-Panzer!*, *The Development of Tank Warfare* (London, Cassell, 1999 [1937]).

that our forces can make themselves ready for the battle, change their crews after the long approach marches, distribute rations and establish contact with other arms ... the objectives of the attack and relevant landmarks should be pointed out to the subordinate commanders on the spot. If this prove impossible ... we resort to the compass.[5]

Between 1916 and 1918 the relative small number of Tank Corps Intelligence and Reconnaissance Officers had an importance out of all proportion to their numbers in British tank operations after September 1916. Sir Winston Churchill, one of the 'fathers' of the tanks, might well have remarked that in the field of tank operations in the Great War that never was so much owed to so few.

5   Ibid., pp. 181-183.

15

Postscript

Both Hotblack and Dillon changed their volunteer status to become regular army officers during and after the war. Frederick Elliot (Boots) Hotblack had a particularly successful military career ending up as a Major General (Temporary) in spite of having only one eye. In 1920 he spent a year at Staff College, Camberley where he was credited with 'Passing Staff College' (psc). In 1922 he was appointed Brigade Major of the 1st Rhine Infantry Brigade, Silesian Forces. The permanent formation of the Royal Tank Corps in1923 led to Hotblack's appointment as a General Staff Officer for military training. On 21 January 1932 he was appointed to the Staff College, Camberley until 19 December 1934. At the College he displayed a 'quiet sense of humour and was a kind and considerate instructor.'[1] He was due to be posted to the Armoured Car Company (ACC) in India but instead he became Military Attaché at the British Embassy in Berlin between 1935 and 1937 and was promoted to Colonel (with seniority) on 5 May 1935. He witnessed demonstrations by the *Wehrmacht* at Kassel which included an all-arms battle involving tanks, anti-tank artillery, the air force, infantry and cavalry.[2] In Germany he forwarded his knowledge of the growing German Panzer Corps to the War Office where it seems to have gathered dust. He was Aide-de-camp to King George VI in 1939 but there is a suggestion that just before the outbreak of the Second World War he returned to Berlin.[3] He was promoted to Brigadier and returned to France for a second time with the British Expeditionary Force on the staff of Field Marshal Sir John Dill. He soon returned home on his appointment as Commander of the 2nd Armoured Division and promotion to temporary Major General preparing to recapture Trondheim during the ill-fated Norwegian Expedition in 1940. But his military career came to a sudden and mysterious conclusion. It was reported that

---

1   At the Staff College his students affectionately called him 'Hotboots. (Davy letter of Appreciation).
2   *The Yorkshire Post*, 8 July 1935.
3   Davy letter.

unfortunately he suffered a serious stroke on the Duke of York (Waterloo) Steps whilst on a visit to the War Office. He was convinced that he had been assaulted perhaps by an enemy agent since the Germans were well aware that he had considerable knowledge about their Panzer tactics through his time in Berlin.

> His memory returned very slowly and for some days he thought that he was in Rouen hospital in 1918. He still had the impression that he had been hit on the head with a softish heavy weapon from behind. Later head operations confirmed that extensive internal bleeding had taken place in the skull. 'Boots' was finally invalided out of the army at the end of 1941.[4]

Medical opinion is that the brain operation would normally treat a subdural haematoma to the surface of the brain which a blow could cause not a stroke which occurs deep inside the brain.[5] The bleeding, of course, could have resulted from hitting his head as he fell. It should also be recalled that he suffered a head injury at Arras and then refused to stay in hospital.

However, he recovered well and remained fit. In his enforced retirement he made important contributions to the controversial debates about the Great War that emerged in the 1960s when anti-war rhetoric was popular. He died at the age of ninety-two on 9 January 1979. Liddell Hart prepared his obituary for the *Times*.

Captain, later Colonel, Norman Musgrave (Mark) Dillon also lived into his nineties. He was fortunate not to have had his foot amputated after the wound he received during the Battle of Amiens became gangrenous. He was transferred to Wandsworth Hospital which he thought 'was the Workhouse converted for the reception of wounded. It was pretty rough, and the staff had all the signs of having been there in the Workhouse days'.[6] However, some parental string-pulling, enabled him to move to Londonderry House where he appreciated 'the comfort and kindness he received there.' After convalescence in Scotland he was posted back to Bovington in November 1918 where he met up again with his brother officers from the 2nd (B) Tank Corps Battalion but had little to do other than await demobilisation. In the meantime he taught in the Reconnaissance Section of the Central School where he had only six trainees and so he spent most of the time rebuilding a small car. However, as has been noted, soon 'the Reconnaissance School was closed up, its need having gone'. It was then that he applied for a Regular Commission. At this time technically there were still no Tank Corps officers since all the officers had been seconded from other regiments. Dillon was still officially an officer in the Northumberland Fusiliers.

---

4   Chadwick, p. 516. This is unreferenced and Hotblack's medical details are withheld by the Army Personnel Centre.
5   This opinion was provided by Dr David Farrugia, Consultant at the Cheltenham General Hospital.
6   BLUL, Record of N. M. Dillon, p. 26.

Major General F.E. Hotblack in 1960. (Geoffrey Hotblack)

Consequently he was gazetted in the Munster Fusiliers but following the partition of Ireland three years later he transferred to the King's (Liverpool) Regiment. When the official formation of the Royal Tank Corps took place, he was automatically posted to this new regiment. He passed his promotional exam and so was quickly restored to the rank of Captain in 1924.

Initially he trained and examined drivers of Rolls Armoured Cars. One driver who passed the test with flying colours was Private Shaw (T.E. Lawrence of Arabia). Apparently, according to Dillon, Shaw/Lawrence staved off boredom in training by taking notes in Arabic. Captain Dillon was posted to the 7th Armoured Car Company first at Peshawar then Lahore, India (now Pakistan) in 1925. He seems to have spent a good deal of time hunting (jackals), shooting (crocodiles) and fishing. He was seriously paralyzed following a hunting accident that damaged his spine and from which he was slow to recover. This was a disability which may have prevented him engaging in frontline service in the Second World War. In 1928 he moved to Army Head Quarters, Delhi to become 'Technical Staff Officer and Tank Engineer'. Here he met up with an old Great War brother officer Archie Halford Walker. One of his tasks was to test new Armoured Cars and Light Tanks on the North West frontier.

In April 1931 he was posted home and was not unhappy to leave India which he found in general to be 'a most unpleasant place'.[7] His postings switched between Catterick in north Yorkshire and Bovington. He married Margaret Munro Ellis, known as 'Jimmie', in November 1935 before being posted to Egypt. Here old RO habits died hard since he 'did a bit of manoeuvring about the desert, and made some maps which I hope but doubt, were put to use in the 2nd War.'[8] In 1936 he was back in the UK now a Major and at the War Office to oversee the development of new weapons. Much time was spent developing a tank with a searchlight that was immune to bullets. He also resurrected an old interest in a compass suitable for use in tanks. In this experimental work he met up again with Major General J.F.C. Fuller and rented a flat from another former RO, John Scrutton.

In 1942 he was a Lieutenant Colonel commanding Training Battalions of the Armoured Corps back at Catterick. Here it was a case of *plus ça change, plus c'est la même chose* since the lack of tanks to undertake this work was similar to that which existed at Elvedon in 1916. His responsibilities led to his promotion to full Colonel and President of No. 15 War Office Selection Board at Tadcaster, Yorkshire. He then volunteered to undertake similar work in Egypt and established No. 1 Middle East Selection Board at Maadi, Cairo. He returned to Egypt following a short visit to the Highland Training Centre commanded by Lord Lovat. He remained in Egypt until 1946.

After the war he saw little further opportunity to gain promotion to brigadier so decided to retire. He returned to his roots in the north-east of England where until 1952 he farmed before finally retiring at the age of 62. He and 'Jimmie' moved to Durham where both made contributions to the community including recording his experiences in both World Wars. He died in 1997 aged 99.

Clough Williams-Ellis was demobilised within two weeks of the Armistice. He used his contacts at home to obtain a post as Superintending Architect at the Ministry of Agriculture. Brigadier General Elles appears to have supported his release on condition that Williams-Ellis wrote a history of the Tank Corps; 'So at last, on the understanding that the book would certainly be produced and quickly, I was released.' He recognized that he had engaged in flagrant lobbying and wire-pulling.[9]

He soon returned to his profession as an architect and 'obtained commissions, by charm, guile and pull'. His most well-known work was the creation of the Italianate village at Portmeirion in 1925. He was busy, prosperous and fashionable and in 1929 he became a Fellow of the Institute of British Architects. He was a life-long champion of conservation which included the establishment of the Campaign for the Preservation of Rural England and Wales. After the Second World War he played an important part in civil planning, especially the creation of New Towns. He was

---

7   NAM, 1987-03-9 and *Dillon Record,* p. 44.
8   Ibid., p. 45.
9   Williams-Ellis, *Architect Errant,* pp. 128-129.

Major Clough Williams-Ellis. (TCWEF)

knighted in 1972. He, like his fellow reconnaissance officer, lived into his nineties dying on 10 April 1978, aged ninety four. His obituary in the *'Times'* described him well both as an architect and Intelligence officer :

> He was remarkable chiefly for himself. With his tall gaunt smiling figure, his idiosyncratic clothes, his innocent but powerful vanity, his sly humour, his appalling spelling, his mandarin handwriting, his rasping angular voice, his very real kindness and his guileless love of gaiety and beauty, Clough Williams-Ellis was his own best work, splendid in all proportions.

Demobilisation did not come quickly for Browne. A week after the Armistice he was posted from the 7th to the 12th Battalion, Tank Corps. In his new battalion Browne joined the British Army of Occupation at the Rhine bridgehead of Cologne. He was eventually demobilised at Crystal Palace on 27 November 1919. During the year he spent nearly a fifth of the time on leave including his demobilisation leave. On two occasions the War Office saw fit to extend his leave, at least once for dental treatment. Following demobilisation Browne resumed his pre-war profession of writer. His first task, whilst his memory was still fresh and his papers available, was to complete his monumental work of 526 pages *The Tank in Action* for Blackwood Press. It was published in 1920 only a year after leaving the army. It is part-history of the Tank

Corps, part-memoir and part-polemic. The 2009 edition added the words *During the First World War* to the title. The following spring he appears to have married Miss Gertrude M. Backus. It seems that, sadly, within the year she had died. Whether as a consequence of this bereavement or not he wrote no more books until 1930. Perhaps it was in happier times that he recommenced his writing after meeting and marrying Gwendolen L. Hibbert in 1932. He had returned to writing in 1930 with his *Uncle William and Other Stories*. Before he died at the age of seventy-nine in 1963 he had written twenty five books in all.[10] His principal genre was crime. He was the author of fourteen crime novels at least one of which drew on his military experience and time in Cologne.[11] His fascination with crime included three biographies of Bernard Spilsbury, the celebrated pathologist, and the Lord Chief Justice Sir Travers Humphreys. He completed a *History of Scotland Yard* and a book about crime detection. Browne added two other non-fiction volumes of military history to his book on tanks. A trawl through second hand book shops or the internet may acquaint the curious reader with some of these volumes.

Acting Captain Basil Lucas Quixano Henriques did not possess the same contacts as Williams-Ellis and therefore was not demobilised until the end of January, 1919. On 31 August 1918 Henriques left the 1st Tank Brigade in Artois and was posted back to Bovington and Swanage to train new Reconnaissance Officers and help to form a new Tank Brigade. He was there at the Armistice. He was demobilised on 22 January 1919 (Army Form Z3) where upon he 'stormed, three steps at a time, up three flights of stairs that led to his one roomed home in Cannon Street Road. He flung off his khaki and demanded his old tweed coat and grey flannel trousers, and sat down to peruse the Boys' Club Attendance Register.'[12]

Although he did not reach the great age of his fellow ROs he received national recognition for his work with the Jewish Community in the East End of London. He lobbied his co-religionists to gain their financial help in building a magnificent Settlement in Berner Street, which was later renamed Henriques Street, off the Commercial Road. He became an authority on working with young people and establishing Youth Clubs. As a magistrate he was greatly concerned with Juvenile courts. On the outbreak of the Second World War his application to re-join the army on active service was turned down on health grounds. He had developed diabetes. He became Commanding Officer of a cadet unit of the Royal Fusiliers based on his Settlement's Boys' Club. The Settlement though was on the front line during the London Blitz where it was both an air raid shelter and centre of Civil defence. When he retired from running the Settlement he was awarded a CBE in 1948 as 'lately Warden of the Bernard Baron Oxford and St. George's Settlement and member of the council of the National Association of Boys' Clubs.' In 1955 he received a knighthood for all

---

10   See Appendix III for Browne's complete works.
11   D.G. Browne, *Plan XVI*, (London, Methuen, 1934).
12   This date conflicts with that given in Loewe, *Basil Henriques*, p. 53.

Captain Basil Henriques and Royal Fusilier Army cadets. (IWM D6535)

his social work in the Anglo-Jewish community and with young people. In the 1950s Henriques' health began to fail. He developed glaucoma and lost the sight of one eye. This was followed by stomach cancer. In 1959 he was suffering from coronary disease. He died of heart failure on 2 December 1961. He was 70-years-old.

In the Settlement there were two memorials commemorating the fallen local Jewish servicemen of both World Wars. The memorials remain in the Jewish Community Centre in Stepney Green although most of the Jewish community now live elsewhere and the Settlement closed. The present writer was privileged to attend the annual memorial service at the invitation of the late Rabbi Lawrence Rigal when the memorial boards were displayed and he read out the names of the Jewish fallen. On the Roll of Honour to the fallen of the First World War alongside the name of Basil's brother Ronald, who was killed on the Aisne in 1914, is that of a gentile: 'G. Macpherson', his close friend and Tank Corps comrade, who died on 15 September 1916 when the tanks went into action for the first time.

The Great War Roll of Honour of the Jewish Fallen which includes the Gentile George Macpherson. (Author)

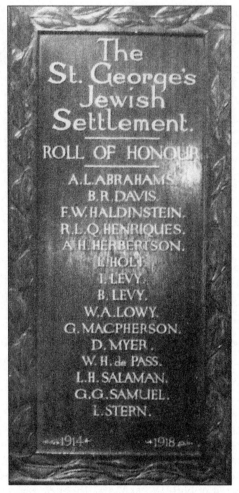

Henriques' own words perhaps provide a suitable epitaph for all the Reconographers.

I came back to England in April 1918 to form a new battalion, the contrast with September 1916 was remarkable with regards to the cooperation of the tanks with other units, the close liaison between the tank commanders and the officers of the infantry, and, above all, the very careful reconnaissance from maps, aeroplane photos, and actual work on the ground itself.[13]

13   Henriques, *The Indiscretions of a Warden*, p. 125.

Appendix I

Regions (PAYS) of France in Which Tanks Operated

PROVINCE	PAYS
A. FLANDERS	French Walloon (Lille)
	Hainault (Valencienne)
	Cambrésis (Cambrai)
B. ARTOIS	Arras
	Gohelle
c. PICARDIE	Amienois (Amiens)
	Santerre (Peronne)
	Vermandois (Saint Quentin)
	Noyonnais (Noyan)

Appendix II

Tank Corps Intelligence and Reconnaissance Officers 1916-18

Capt. F. A. Alker
2/Lt. J. M. Bailey MC & Bar
Capt. B. S. Beale MC
Capt. J. P. Black
2/Lt. A. H. C. Borger MC
Capt. B. J. F. Bradbeer
Lieut. J. Brown MC
Capt. D. G. Browne MC
Capt. Butterworth
Capt. J. Carson
2/Lt B. S. Carter MC & Bar
Capt. R. de Cazalet MC
Capt. S. M. Cook
Major R. F. Cooper
Capt. W. E. Demutt
Lieut. S. Doward
Lieut. R. L. H. de Thierry MC
Capt. D. M. Dillon MC
Capt. H. L. Elton MC
Capt. C. G. Fane
Capt. E. J. Hobbs
Lieut. R. A. Gatfield
2/Lt K. Gordon
Capt. E. Guillaume MC
Capt. A. P. F. Hamilton MC
Capt. B. Handford
Capt. H. C. Hatton-Hall MC
Capt. B. L. Q. Henriques It. Sil. Med.
Capt. G. A. Herberts MC
Capt. H. H. Hindmarsh

Major F. E. Hotblack DSO & Bar, MC & Bar
Capt. J. C. Jinks
2/Lt. J. E. Jones
Lieut. J. D. Kennedy MC
Capt. R. C. Knight MC & Bar
Capt. G. D. C. Koe
Lieut. R. H. Ledger MC
Capt. J. L. Lees MC
Capt. C. H. Lindsay
Capt. McBean
2/Lt. R. C. McNicol
Lieut. T. M. Micklem
Capt. D. L. Monagham
2/Lt. J. M. Morley
Capt. T. A. Nelson
Capt. C. North MC
2/Lt. C. E. Parr
Lieut. T. E. Prentice MC
Lieut. G. A. Prescott MC
Capt. D. T. Raikes MC & Bar
Capt. G. K. Ransom
2/Lt. W. Robinow MC
Capt. N. J. Samson
Lieut. C. L. Saul
Capt. E. C. H. Shillaker
Capt. A. E. S. Scrutton
2/Lt. E. A. Smith MC
Capt. R. C. Snewing
Capt. R. Spencer MC
Capt. J. R. Stanford
Capt. D. B. Swinton
Capt. R. J. K. Ap Thomas
Lieut. C. R. Thornback MC
Major F. Tucker MC
2/Lt. F. C. Walker MC
Capt. J. Westcott MC
Capt. A. M. Whyte
Lieut. E. Whiteside MC
Major C. Williams-Ellis MC
Capt. L. Wilson
Capt. B. N. Woole
Capt. C. P. Voss MC & Bar

Appendix III

The books of (Captain) Douglas Gordon Browne by genre[1]

Crime

Novels
The Dead Don't Bite, (London, Methuen & Co., 1933)
The Cotfold Conundrums, (London, Methuen & Co., 1933)
Plan XVI, (London, Methuen & Co., 1934)
The Looking Glass' Murders, (London, Methuen & Co., 1935)
The Stolen Boat Train, (London, Methuen &Co., 1935)
The May Week Murders, (London, Methuen & Co., 1937)
The House of the Sword, (London, Hutchinson & Co., 1939)
Death Wears a Mask, (London, Hutchinson & Co., 1940)
Too Many Cousins, (London, Macdonald & Co., 1946)
What Beckoning Ghost, (London, Macdonald & Co., 1947)
Rustling End, (London, Macdonald & Co., 1948)
Death in Perpetuity, (London, Macdonald & Co., 1950)
Sergeant Death, (London, Macdonald & Co., 1955)
Death in Seven Volumes, (London, Macdonald & Co., 1958

Non-Fiction
Bernard Spilsbury: His Life and Cases, (London, George G. Harrap, 1951)
Fingerprints: Fifty Years of Crime Detection, Alan Brook, 1954)
Bernard Spilsbury: His Life and Cases, (London, Hamilton & Co., 1955) and Eric
    Vivian Tullett (with some deletions).
The Rise of Scotland Yard. A History of the Metropolitan Police, (London, George G.
    Harrap, 1956)
Sir Travers Humphery: a Biography, (George G. Harrap & Co., 1960

---

1   British Library (BL), catalogue

Bernard Spilsbury: His Life and Cases, (London, Hamilton & Co., 1963) with Eric Vivian Tullett

Military
The Tank in Action, (London, Blackwood, 1920)
Private Thomas Atkins: A History of the British Soldier from 1840 to 1940, (London, Hutchinson & Co., 1940)
The Floating Bulwarks; the Story of the Fighting Ship, (London, Cassell, 1963)

Miscellaneous
Christ and His Age, (London, Methuen & Co., 1913)
Uncle William and Other Stories, (London, Blackwood & Co., 1930)

Bibliography

Primary Sources including Published Memoirs

Army Personnel Centre, Support Division Historical Disclosures, Glasgow. B.L.Q. Henriques and F.E.Hotblack papers.

Baker-Carr, C. B. *From Chauffeur to Brigadier* (London, Ernest Benn Ltd., 1930).

Dillon, N. M., Liddle Collection, University of Leeds, GS 0459.

Foot, S, *Three Lives,* (London, William Heinemann Ltd., 1934).

Fuller, J. F. C., *Memoirs of an Unconventional Soldier* (London, Ivor Nicholson & Watson Ltd., 1936).

General Staff, *SS135 Instruction for the Training of Divisions for Offensive Action (December 1916).*

—— *SS164 Notes on the Use of Tanks and the general principles of their* employment *as an adjunct to the Infantry attack* (1917).

—— *SS203, Instructions for Anti-Tank Defence (Provisional),* (February, 1918).

—— *SS204 Infantry and Tank Co-operation and Training* (March 1918).

Henriques, B. L. Q., Report dated 17. 9.1916, Bovington Tank Museum and Archives, Henriques box

—— Attack on the Quadrilateral (transcriptionof a lecture delivered 6 March 1917,) Bovington Tank Museum Archives.

—— *The Indiscretions of a Warden* (London, Methuen & Co. Ltd., 1937).

Hickey, D. E., *Rolling into Action. Memoirs of a Tank Corps Section Commander* (Uckfield, The Naval & Military Press Ltd. Reprint (2007 [internal evidence suggests that it was originally published in the early 1930s]).

Intelligence Corps Archive, Hotblack Papers, Chicksand, Beds.

IWM., Interview with Dillon, Norman Musgrave, catalogue number 8752, 1987.

Liddell Hart Archive, Kings College, London, Hotblack-Fuller papers.

Tank Corps HQ, Instructions for the Training of the Tank Corps in France (1 December 1917.

NAM, Holford-Walker Papers, 32383.

—— Memoirs of the army service of Col. Norman Musgrave Dillon, 1987-03-9.

The National Archives (Kew)

    WO 95/100, 1st Bde., 7nd Bat., May 1917.

    WO 95/101, 2nd Bde., HQ., Feb.-Dec. 1917.

WO 95/104, 3rd Bde., HQ., Apr.-Dec. 1917.

WO 95/106, 3rd Bde., 3rd., Bat., Apr.1917-Mar. 1919.

WO 95/108, 4th Bde., HQ. Dec. 1917-Mar. 1919.

WO 95/110, 4th Bde., D. Coy, Aug. 1916-Sept. 1917.

WO 95/113, 5th Bde., 2nd Bat., May 1917.

WO 95/118, 6th Bde., Training Centres, 1917.

WO 158/832, Tanks and their Employment and Cooperation with other Arms

WO 158/836, Tank HQ.

WO 158/837, Charteris.

WO 158/849, Branch and Services Organisation 01 November 1918-31 January 1920.

War Office, *Field Service Regulations, Part 1, Operations 1909 (Reprinted with Amendments, 1912* (London, HMSO, 1912).

Watson, W. H. L., *A Company of Tanks* (Uckfield, The Naval & Military Press & London, Imperial War Museum, undated).

Williams-Ellis, C., *Architect Errant* (London, Constable & Co. 1971).

Secondary Sources: Journal articles & Research Papers

Balchin, W. G. V., 'Graphicacy Should be the Fourth Ace in the Pack', *The Cartographer*, 1966, pp. 23-28 and 'Graphicacy', *Geography*, 57 (1972), pp. 185-195.

Beach, James, 'British Intelligence and German Tanks'1916-1918, *War in History*, vol. 14.4, pp. 454-475.

Beach, James, 'British Intelligence and the German Army, 1914-1918', (PhD thesis, University College London, 2004).

Chadwick, Ken, '"Boots" The Call for Service', *The Tank*, vol. 57, 1974.

Doyle, Peter, 'Geology and War on the Western Front, 1914-18', *Geology Today*, Vol. 30, no. 5, September-October 2014.

Doyle, Peter & Bennett, Matthew R., Military Geography: terrain evaluation and the British western Front 1914-18, The Geographical Journal, vol. 163, part 1, March, 1997.

Hammond, C. B.,'The Theory and Practice of Tank Cooperation with Other Arms on the Western Front during the First World War' (PhD. thesis, Birmingham University, 2005).

Hardy Colin, 'Rewriting History-An Alternative Account of the Death of Lieutenant George Macpherson of the Heavy Section Machine Gun Corps', *Stand To! The Journal of the Western Front Association*, August/September 2010, Number 89.

Jones, S., 'Scouting for Soldiers, Reconnaissance and the British Cavalry 1899-1914', *War in History*, 18 (4), 2011, pp. 495-513).

Mitchell, C. W. & Gavish, D., 'Land on Which Battles are Won or Lost', *Geographical Magazine*, 52, 1980.

Travers, T., 'Could the Tanks of 1918 Been War Winners for the British Expeditionary Force?', *Journal of Contemporary History, vol. 27, (1992)*.

Printed Sources

Barnett, C., *The Swordbearers, Supreme Command in the First World War* (London, Cassell & Co, 2000 [1963]).

Barton, P. with Banning, J., *Arras* (London, Constable, 2010).

Beach, J., 'Scouting for Brigands: British Tank Corps and Intelligence, 1916-18' in Searle, A. (ed) *Genesis, Employment, Aftermath: First World War Tanks and the New Warfare* (Solihull, Helion Company Ltd., 2015).

Beach, James, *Haig's Intelligence, GHQ and the German Army*, (Cambridge University Press, 2013)

Blair, Dale, *The Battle of Bellicourt Tunnel*, (Frontline Books, London, 2011).

Bloom, B. S. (ed.), *Taxonomy of Educational Objectives, Handbook I, The Cognitive Domain*, (London, Longman, Green & Co., 1955).

Boff, Jonathan, *Winning and Losing on the Western Front*,(Cambridge University Press, 2012).

Browne, D. G., *The Tank in Action During the First World War* (Edinburgh, Blackwood & Sons,1920).

Campbell, C., *Band of Brigands* (London, Harper Press, 2007.)

Chasseaud, P. & Doyle, P., *Grasping Gallipoli: Terrain, Maps and Failure at the Dardanelles, 1915* (Stroud, Spellmount, The History Press, 2015 [2005]).

Clausewitz, C. von, *On War* (Oxford, University Press, 2007).

Cooper, B., *The Ironclads of Cambrai* (Barnsley, Pen & Sword Military, 2010 [1967]).

Doherty, R., & Chapman, R., *The British Reconnaissance in World War II*, (Oxford, Osprey Publishing Ltd., 2007.

Fletcher, D., *The British Tanks 1915-19* (Marlborough, Crowood Press Ltd., 2001).

—— (ed.), *Tanks and Trenches* (Stroud, Sutton Publishing Ltd., undated).

Foley, J., *The Boilerplate War* (London, Fredrick Muller, 1963).

Fuller, J. F. C., *Tanks in the Great War 1914-1918* (Uckfield, Naval & Military Press Ltd, reprint, 1919).

Gibot, J.L.& Gorczynski, P., *Follow the Tanks, Cambrai, 20 November-7 December 1917* (Arras, Imprimerie Centrale de l'Artois, trans. McAdam, W., 1999).

'Graphite', *Reconography: Simplified Reconnaissance Sketching*, (London, Hodder & Stoughton, 1920).

Griffith, Paddy, *Forward into Battle*, (Swindon, Croward Press, 1990 [1981].

Guderian, Heinz, *Achtung-Panzer! The Development of Tank Warfare,* (London, Cassell, 1999 [1937]).

Hammond, C.B., *Cambrai 1917* (London, Weiderfeld & Nicolson, 2008).

Harris, J. P., *Men, Ideas and Tanks, British military thought and `armoured forces, 1903-1939* (Manchester, Manchester University, 1995).

—— 'The Rise of Armour' in Griffith, P. (ed), *British Fighting Methods in the Great War* (London: Frank Cass, 1996).

—— & Barr, N., *Amiens to the Armistice: The BEF in the Hundred Days Campaign, 8 August-11 November* (London, Brassey's, 1998).

—— 'Haig and the Tank', in Bond, B & Cave, N., eds, *Haig: A Reappraisal 80 Years On* (Barnsley, Pen & Sword Military, 2009 [1999]).

Henderson, D., *The Art of Reconnaissance* (London, John Murray, 1915 [1907]).

Henderson, G. F. R., *The Science of War-a Collection of Essays And Lectures 1891-1903* (London, Longmans, Green, and Co., 1912 [1905]).

Kershaw, R., *Tank Men* (London, Hodder & Stoughton Ltd., 2008.

Liddell Hart, B. H., *The Tanks, the History of the Royal Tank Regiment and its Predecessors, Vol. 1, 1914-1939* (London, Cassell, 1959).

LoCicero, Michael, *A Moonlight Massacre, The Night Operation on the Passchendaele Ridge, 2 December 1917* (Solihull, Helion & Company Ltd., 2014).

Loewe, L. L., *Basil Henriques, A Portrait* (London, Routledge & Kegan Paul, 1976).

Maurice, R. F. G. (ed.), *Tank Corps Book of Honour* (Uckfield, The Naval & Military Press Ltd., 1919 reprint).

Miles, W., *Military Operations France and Belgium 1916, Vol. 2* (Uckfield, Naval and Military Press reprint [1938].

Mitchell, Colin, *Terrain Evaluation* (London, Longmans Group Ltd., 1973).

Mitchell, F., *Tank Warfare, The Story of the Tanks in the Great War* (London, Thomas Nelson and Sons Ltd., 1933, Naval & Military Press Ltd., reprint, undated).

Occleshaw, M., *Armour Against fate British Military Intelligence in the First World War* (London, Columbus Books Ltd, 1989).

Palazzo, A., *Seeking Victory on the Western Front* (Lincoln & London, University of Nebraska Press, 2000).

Parritt, B., *The Intelligencers, British Military Intelligence from the Middle Ages to 1929* (Barnsley, Pen & Sword Military, 2011).

Peaple, Simon, *Mud, Blood and Determination; the History of the 46th (North Midland) Division in the Great War* (Solihull, Helion & Co. Ltd., 2015).

Pidgeon, T., *Tanks at Flers* (Cobham, Fairmile Books, 1995).

—— *Tanks on the Somme: From Morval to Beaumont Hamel* (Barnsley, Pen & Sword Military, 2010).

Prior R. & Wilson T., *Passchendaele, The Untold Story* (New Haven and London, Yale University Press, 2002 [1996]).

Sheffield, G. D., *Forgotten Victory* (London, Headline Book Publishing, 2002 [2001]).

—— *The Chief, Douglas Haig and the British Army* (London, Aurum Press, 2011).

Senior, Michael, *Haking: A Dutiful Soldier, Barnsley* (Pen& Sword Military, 2012).

Simkins, P., 'Somme Reprise: Reflections on the Fighting for Albert and Bapaume', in Bond, B., et al., *Look to your Front: Studies in the First World War by the British Commission for Military History* (Staplehurst, Spellmount, 1999).

Somers, Lord, *The War History of the Sixth Tank Battalion* (privately published, 1919, reprinted Naval & Military press, undated).

Swinton, E. D., *Eyewitness* (London, Hodder and Stoughton, 1932).

Trythall, A. J., *Boney Fuller, The Intellectual General* (London, Cassell, 1977).

Sun Tzu, *The Art of War* (London: Pax Librorum Publishing House, 2009).

Vans, Jamie & Widderson, Peter (eds), Veteran Volunteer (Barnsley, Pen & Sword Military, 2014.

Verrinder, I., *Tank Action in the Great War, B Battalion's Experiences 1917* (Barnsley, Pen & Sword Military, 2009).

Walker, J., *The Blood Tub, General Gough and the Battle of Bullecourt 1917* (Staplehurst, Spellmount, 2000).

Williams-Ellis, C. & A., *The Tank Corps* (Country Life, 1919).

Woollcombe, R., *First Tank Battle: Cambrai 1917* (London, Arthur Barker, Ltd., 1967).

Wylly, H. C., *History of the 1st & 2nd Battalions The Leicestershire Regiment in the Great War* (Aldershot, Gale & Polden Ltd., undated).

Zabecki, D. T., *The German 1918 Offensive (Strategy and History)*, (Abingdon, Routledge, 2006).

Index

INDEX OF PEOPLE

INDEX OF PLACES

INDEX OF MILITARY UNITS & FORMATIONS

INDEX OF GENERAL & MISCELLANEOUS TERMS

Wolverhampton Military Studies

www.helion.co.uk/wolverhamptonmilitarystudies

Submissions

The publishers would be pleased to receive submissions for this series. Please contact us via email (info@helion.co.uk), or in writing to Helion & Company Limited, 26 Willow Road, Solihull, West Midlands, B91 1UE.

Titles

No.1 *Stemming the Tide. Officers and Leadership in the British Expeditionary Force 1914* Edited by Spencer Jones (ISBN 978-1-909384-45-3)

No.2 *'Theirs Not To Reason Why'. Horsing the British Army 1875–1925* Graham Winton (ISBN 978-1-909384-48-4)

No.3 *A Military Transformed? Adaptation and Innovation in the British Military, 1792–1945* Edited by Michael LoCicero, Ross Mahoney and Stuart Mitchell (ISBN 978-1-909384-46-0)

No.4 *Get Tough Stay Tough. Shaping the Canadian Corps, 1914–1918* Kenneth Radley (ISBN 978-1-909982-86-4)

No.5 *A Moonlight Massacre: The Night Operation on the Passchendaele Ridge, 2 December 1917. The Forgotten Last Act of the Third Battle of Ypres* Michael LoCicero (ISBN 978-1-909982-92-5)

No.6 *Shellshocked Prophets. Former Anglican Army Chaplains in Interwar Britain* Linda Parker (ISBN 978-1-909982-25-3)

No.7 *Flight Plan Africa: Portuguese Airpower in Counterinsurgency, 1961–1974* John P. Cann (ISBN 978-1-909982-06-2)

CPSIA information can be obtained
at www.ICGtesting.com
Printed in the USA
BVOW06*1037071216

469894BV00004B/12/P